AS LUCK WOULD HAVE IT

RANDOM THOUGHTS, MUSINGS AND MEMORIES

PADMANABHA ARKALGUD

(AS TOLD TO VANI SUKUMAR)

INDIA • SINGAPORE • MALAYSIA

ISBN 979-8-89277-280-8

Luck is believing you're lucky— Tennessee Williams

CONTENTS

Acknowledgements *VII*

Preface *IX*

1. To the Southern Tip of the World 1
2. Flashes From the Early Years 8
3. From the College Years 29
4. The Learning Curve 45
5. Managing Risks and Challenges 58
6. On the Job and on the Move 71
7. From the Guntur Diaries 85
8. The Stint in Bangalore 98
9. The Bhadrachalam Days 118
10. Life After ITC 154
11. Around the World 164
12. In Conclusion 184

About The Author *187*

Acknowledgements

This book has its genesis in the imagination and commitment of my younger sister, Vani Sukumar.

Listening to my life stories during casual conversations over the years, she felt the need to put them down on paper and suggested that I narrate my experiences over the telephone every morning, which she would record and later transcribe. This process continued till I felt I had shared all that needed to be said.

Meanwhile, Vani stitched the narrative together in a sequence and sent me the transcripts. It was truly a labour of love—done with utmost care and diligence.

One cannot thank her enough for her effort. God bless her!

Thanks are also due to Vani's husband, Sukumar Gonibeed and their son Ananth and daughter Aparna for their invaluable support. Also, Ebeneser Paul and all of Vani's secretarial staff for their dedicated assistance. We are both equally indebted to Smt. Prasanna Ramesh, Smt. Anandi Sivakumar and Ms Sarasa for all the help extended.

Pushpa Girimaji, my sister-in-law, and my brother A. Surya Prakash, both nationally acclaimed media persons, read the manuscript and gave valuable suggestions. Thank you for sparing the time and effort.

My wife, Uma, deserves a round of applause for her silent support and the extraordinary patience she showed throughout this journey. She has been a pillar of strength ever since our marriage fifty years ago and has been a witness to many events in my life.

Gratitude is due to my friend Dr G.K. Jayaram, first chairman of Infosys, who gave me this valuable, pithy and down to earth advice: "Tell your story, but don't preach."

Last but not the least, a round of thanks to Shubhomoy Sikdar who edited the original manuscript and gave valuable advice on the narration and the sequencing of chapters. His professional touch, sharp eye for detail and editing skills transformed the contents of this book into a publishable product.

Preface

Does age matter? If you ask me, it does.

I am not merely referring to the physical and bodily manifestations of the process of ageing. These are the obvious and visible changes that nature brings about as we log in the years. I have 86 years behind me.

But our sojourn on Planet Earth counts at another level which is more than skin deep or physical. You could call it the wisdom that one acquires and accumulates from lived experiences. This learning, which encompasses both failures and success is unique to each individual and can provide valuable insights once processed, assimilated, and shared.

One occasionally comes across a percipient interpretation of life when a person with the gravitas and sobriety of experience recalls an incident from his or her life. It often sets us thinking and holds our attention because of the relevance the narrative has in our own lives. Unfortunately, the recollections have limited reach and do not go beyond the immediate family or friend circle of the narrator. Indeed, for all practical purposes they are lost to the world.

This truth was driven home to me by my sister, Vani. She used to listen enthralled by my reminiscences, but one day she urged me to be more than a colourful and insightful raconteur. "You have to put it down in writing," she said. Till then I had never considered penning my thoughts or recording the events that shaped my life.

However, since Vani was insistent, I agreed. We worked out a plan to make the book project possible. It went something like this: She would call me each morning at 6.30 from Chennai and I would narrate my experiences chapter by chapter (or episode by episode, as I put it) and she would record it on her phone. She would later playback the audio and transcribe it on her laptop and send me a draft copy to read. In this manner, courtesy the internet, my book slowly began to take shape.

As the story unfolded, I realized that my readers would indeed profit from my experiences. For example, one of the lessons life taught me was that you will always find a solution provided you don't give up. Help and inspiration will be forthcoming provided you don't declare yourself overwhelmed and defeated. Indeed, looking back I can say with a measure of pride that whenever I was confronted with a problem, I always found a way out. This was because I looked for a solution and that kept my mind focussed.

Professor Ramachandran, who is no more, was my teacher and mentor when I was a student at the Tata Institute of Social Sciences, Bombay. In his very first lecture the good professor shared this nugget of wisdom with his students: "What is permanent in life is change. Don't get ruffled or disturbed by change that takes place day in and day out. The minute there is change you should ask yourself 'what am I going to do about it, does it require a solution?'..."

Professor Ramachandran's words have remained with me ever since and has served me like a mantra of sorts. I have time and again found solutions based on the very thought process that he espoused to us so many years ago.

Similarly, there was a slice of wisdom which came courtesy my father which I dearly still cherish. To put it in context I must go back to my student days when I fancied a career in theatre and totally neglected my studies. The stage was all I cared about as if nothing else mattered. When you are young you set yourself goals to achieve without weighing the pros and cons.

It was at that critical juncture that my father decided to have a heart-to-heart chat with his son. "What do you want to do in life—theatre, or do you wish to pursue education?' he asked.

I was completely taken aback by his question. Till then I had never thought about my future. But after weighing the options before me I decided to continue my education and relegated theatre to the status of a hobby. Later in life, whenever I was caught in two minds, I would ask myself the same question my father had asked me—what do I want? That helped me not only gain clarity but also helped me focus and prioritise my efforts.

By now you may be wondering if this is one of those books offering maxims to follow and formulas to help you lead a meaningful and contended life. Fear not. You have my solemn assurance that in the pages that follow there are no presumptions, sermons or magic mantras from Saint Padmanabha!

Instead, I have laid bare events which have had a profound impact on my life. Some are witty, a few tragic and others spiced with adventure. But in the main they give you a generous and often critical peep into my march through time. It is for you to interpret these tales and glean whatever is worthy from them.

So, please feel free to dip into this book at random. I have not spared any effort to make the contents engaging and entertaining. Indeed, I would suggest you read it from cover to cover!

January, 2024

Bengaluru

I

To the Southern Tip of the World

Even as I write this, I am all of 86 years of age.

When I sat at home in Bangalore and planned a trip to Antarctica in 2014, I was 78. I remember when I first broached the idea of travelling to the southern tip of Planet Earth, many of my friends and near ones wondered if it was prudent on my part—at that age— to venture on such a journey.

There were many who cautioned me about the cold in the polar region and the health problems I might encounter. The summer temperatures, I knew, rarely exceeded minus 20 degrees Celsius except in the coastal regions where it comes up to zero degrees Celsius or thereabout.

I must admit that no one was being unreasonable when they wondered whether such an adventure was worth taking the risk.

But the apprehensions expressed by my well-wishers, instead of acting as a deterrent, only made me more determined to venture forth. I attribute this penchant for taking risks to my upbringing, my nature, and the lessons my varied life experiences taught me.

When I set my sights on Antarctica, I realized that physically I would have to strengthen myself. The apartment in Bangalore where I lived had a gym upstairs. I got hold of the instructor and asked him for some tips. He told me that I did not need to use any of the muscle strengthening machines and devices used by the young. Walking, he advised, would serve me well enough. He also gave me some dietary instructions that included adding goat's head soup and eggs to my diet. When I told him I was a strict vegetarian, he advised me to drink milk and increase my intake of vegetables. He taught me some breathing exercises and I followed this regimen for two months before the journey.

Dear reader, I must confess at this point that I am one of those who believe that in life an out of the blue opportunity rarely presents itself. And any opportunity which fulfils a lingering desire for exploration is not to be missed. If you seize it, it could turn out to be a once-in-a-lifetime divine experience which will be exciting as well as enlightening.

I had not suddenly stumbled on the Antarctica idea. Neither had anyone suggested the trip. It was triggered by an advertisement I saw in an international magazine announcing a fifteen-day sea trip to Antarctica commencing from the port town of Ushuaia in Argentina. The town has long been known as the southern-most city in the world and is one of the five destinations from where one can travel by sea to Antarctica. From Ushuaia the distance to the southern polar region is a little over 1000 km.

I responded to the advertisement and later I discovered that a trip to the Frozen Continent was well within the realm of probability. Some 34,000 tourists had visited Antarctica in the 2012-2013 season. So, my journey would be a lot more organized and structured unlike those early explorers who had to navigate rough seas to sight the land of ice.

The Seattle-based Quark Expeditions, which had advertised the trip, was a company that specialized in conducting Antarctic and Arctic trips. In fact, Quark had the distinction of taking the first group of 'commercial travellers' to the North Pole in 1991. However, the first expedition to Antarctica with travellers, rather than explorers, was in 1966 and was led by a gentleman named Lars Eric Lindblad. The modern expedition cruise industry was born shortly after, in 1969.

I decided to book a ticket on the Quark Expeditions trip. Since my wife Uma did not think that she could withstand the sea journey, I decided I would do it alone. But my son Anand, who was based in Seattle, was keen to join me. He said that this was an opportunity he did not wish to miss since it was unlikely that he would embark on such a journey in the future. So, two berths were booked on the Quark Expeditions' ship from Ushuaia. The Antarctica cruise cost me Rs 1.4 lakh all told.

As part of my first leg of the journey I flew with Uma to Seattle. The plan was to leave her there with my son's family, while Anand and I would fly to Buenos Aires, Argentina's capital, and then on to Ushuaia. We set out in early December—the exact date eludes me since I did not keep a log and my memory is a little foggy about that detail.

We reached the picturesque port town of Ushuaia with the Martial Mountains overlooking it on one side and the Beagle Channel on the other. We were both excited as our plane touched down and we were received at the airport by the staff of Quark Expeditions. They took us to a guest house where we relaxed and did a bit of sightseeing. In the evening the organisers held a special session explaining what precautions we would have to take, who will take care of whom, cabin arrangements on the ship, and what kind of clothing was suited to the weather in Antarctica.

We were also briefed on the facilities available, arrangements for food, and the medical support on the ship for the duration of the eleven day up and down voyage. We were asked to brace ourselves for the fourth and fifth day of our voyage when we would navigate through the Drake Passage, a treacherous stretch of sea between South America's Cape Horn and the South Shetlands Islands of Antarctica.

We were told to hope for "smooth sailing" although conditions were quite unpredictable in the Drake Passage with no landmass to resist the waves. We were told that on choppy days the waves could rise to over 40 feet. However, the first four days would be relatively calmer and enjoyable.

The second afternoon at Ushuaia was billed as 'embarkment day' when we would set sail. The next three days of the journey was a glorious and surreal experience. The ship was like a floating island with chilly winds whizzing past. Several types of curious birds flew parallel to the dock as if to size up the humans on board. Sunrise and sunsets from the ship's deck was a view to behold and the colours changing hues was almost as if nature was showcasing her artistic skills for our benefit. Each sunrise and sunset were unique in their own way.

Since we had been warned, we braced ourselves for the two days that it would take to traverse the Drake Passage. The sea was indeed rough, and the ship rolled and pitched. We had been advised to stay calm, take the medicines which stops nausea and sea sickness if necessary, and to remain in our cabins. If any of us had stomach upsets, we were to contact the ship's doctor.

On the very first evening through the Drake Passage, I had an upset stomach, but the doctor advised me to ignore the symptoms, which I did, and they thankfully subsided. The ship's crew personally ensured each of the passenger's needs were taken care of. We were 560 of us from all over the world speaking different languages and with different food habits. But the ship's crew managed us very well and kept us in good spirits.

Once we crossed the Drake Passage, the Antarctic Sea lay before us calm and serene. This is where our real journey began because we soon reached a point where the ship would drop anchor and the crew would take us in batches of eight to ten passengers to explore the land laden with ice.

We had earlier been provided special boots, water proof caps and raincoats that we had to wear in Antarctica. Of course, we had to wear three layers of clothing and thermals to ward off the cold. So fully geared up we were taken in batches in inflated boats. It was a daily routine we followed as we explored different land portions or islands before returning to the ship.

On the first day I and my son went in the same batch. In the inflated boat there were ten of us and a guide. It took us about an hour to touch land. I remember asking our young guide what would happen to me if I fell into the water and did not know how to swim. He jokingly replied, "Uncle you don't worry, if you fall in the Antarctica waters you will yourself come up after three days." We all had a good laugh over that.

When we touched land, we were simply overwhelmed and humbled by the large structures of ice that we had only seen from a distance so far. It was awe inspiring as if we were in a gigantic art gallery where a celestial sculptor or architect had displayed his or her creations carved from towering blocks of ice. Some of these works of art, I thought, were as tall as the Empire State Building, perhaps even taller. Some were shaped like our own Parliament building in New Delhi or like a giant Shivlinga. Indeed, there were myriad shapes and sizes that dominated the landscape, each as mesmerizing as the other.

And amidst this white landscape, which looked deceptively barren, was a wide variety of wildlife. Other than penguins we associate with the southern hemisphere, particularly Antarctica, there were seals and many species of birds which I could not identify but I could vouch for the fact that they were bright and beautiful. Some of then flew in and out of the cavities, nooks and crannies that naturally formed in the glaciers.

A typical day would begin with breakfast. Then we would take the boat around 9:00 a.m. and return around noon after visiting one or two islands. Lunch was on board the ship and around 2.30 p.m. it was time to set off for another set of islands and return to the ship. In the evening we all had tea followed by a session where we shared what we had seen and learnt.

Though my son had initially accompanied me on the daily excursions, I noticed that I was cramping him because he felt he had to look after me and keep a watch on my activities. He obviously thought I was old and couldn't be as active as he was. I saw that he was often keen to venture further on the icy land where it took more effort to take every step. But with a father to look after he couldn't explore as much as he would have liked.

So, I told him that I had made friends of my own and he could go with his own friends while I would go with mine. He agreed and let himself loose. I had my own group with whom I could hang out and give them little incentives like treating them to the Indian pickles that I had carried with me. You always make friends through such gestures. My fellow passengers from Africa simply loved my pickle!

One thing I noticed about penguins was that they were very possessive about the rocks and pebbles they collected. They built their nests on the iceless ground and they were overprotective of each of the little stones that they gathered and fought among themselves for their possession. Apparently pebbles and rocks also come in handy when the male woos a female. And those who can't find the right pebble steal it from others which can lead to fights. Through my trip I shot videos which I would later show to school children to enlighten them about life in Antarctica.

It is said that you discover something new every day that you spend in Antarctica. I found this to be fascinatingly true. You also learn a lot. This land, far away from civilization as we know it, makes you introspect. Nature seems to be communicating to you through the silence, the cracking sound of the glaciers and the antics of the penguins marching about and squabbling over the pebbles they collected.

One of the life lessons I learnt on the trip was that age is not a hurdle for you to explore the world. Another humbling thought that came to my mind was that I did not know everything I should know. Every time you travel there are things you learn: how beings live differently and in communion with nature. How they struggle with the elements and more than often emerge victorious.

When we said goodbye to Antarctica and made the passage back to Ushuaia, I knew I had witnessed and experienced something remarkable that would remain etched in my memory. As I waved my goodbye to the land, I knew I was carrying back with me images to be cherished. And thoughts I must distil into words.

II

Flashes From the Early Years

As I have recounted, whenever I looked at the vast Antarctic landscape, I was awed by its majesty and rugged charm. Bathed in the stillness of the silence and so close to nature, my mind would at times begin to wander. I would unknowingly embark on a journey into the past. In my mind's eye I could see a kaleidoscope of images, thoughts, fragments of dreams and memories bathed in sepia-tone by the passage of time. Someone has wisely said that if you carry your childhood with you, you never grow old.

Indeed, I felt younger and energized as I luxuriated in my memories which flitted like a butterfly from one incident I recollected to the other. When one reminiscences with a free mind, thoughts come like they do in a stream of consciousness novel. One thought leads to another not in a logical or chronological flow but almost as if it has a mind of its own. So, an incident which happened when you were twenty-five might make you ponder about a story your father told you when you were six. Or a thought that struck you as a teenager would dovetail with an observation you made as an adult. Sometimes you wonder if the randomness of memories recollected in tranquillity has some natural symmetry. It perhaps has but is difficult to fathom.

As I settle down to refine my memories into the written word, I am not sure if I should structure them in a chronological order or let it flow with the natural randomness with which I recall them. I opt for the latter since that would represent them better than any contrived narrative structure. Of course, at the end of the exercise I could perhaps arrange them loosely in an order to give it the shape of a narrative.

So, let me embark on my journey and start by remembering something that my father told me which I often ponder about. Perhaps he narrated this experience hoping that I would profit from it and become all the wiser for it.

From my Father's Book of Experience

In the new millennium Bengaluru, you would only commute the 6 km from Malleswaram to the Majestic Area by bus, car, scooter, auto or by Uber. No one thinks of walking through the crowded streets. But back in the day when he was studying in inter-science, my father used to walk barefoot from his home to the Majestic Area.

One day while he was returning from college, he found a beggar in tattered clothes seeking alms. My father instinctively felt that the person deserved help. He wanted to pay him some money. But when he rummaged through his pocket, he found he had only one coin—and that too a four anna silver coin which he felt was too much to give away.

He was perhaps not unreasonable in thinking so. Before inflation sent prices shooting sky high and the value of money plummeting to the depths, four annas (25 paisa) had considerable buying power. For example, father used to tell us a good vegetarian meal cost no more than an anna. So, parting with four annas as alms was unheard of those days.

I am sure most readers would have heard similar stories from their elders about the buying power of a rupee or a fifty paise coin in the good old days. Anyway, my father thought it prudent not to part with the coin. In fact, as he walked home, he kept rolling it in the palm of his hand inside the pocket to assure himself that it was safe.

But was he right in curbing his initial instinct to help? As he continued walking my father was caught in a dilemma. 'To give or not to give' was the question. He mulled over it for a while and then reasoned that he was being selfish and stingy. He felt sheepish because the realization dawned on him that he had suppressed his overwhelming desire to help a poor and deserving man and had held on to the coin only because of its commercial value.

He decided to turn back and give the coin to the beggar. To his dismay the man had disappeared from the spot where he had earlier found him. My father then spent almost half the day searching for the man in the vicinity. But he could not be found anywhere. He had simply disappeared

Father said he realized with a sense of remorse that his selfishness had robbed him of an opportunity given by God to be of help to a fellow human being. He said there was a lesson that he learnt from this experience which he shared with us.

Giving, he pointed out, was an opportunity, not a sacrifice. 'If you are in a position from which your words or deeds can help others, don't miss the opportunity God has given you,' he said, 'If you miss it, think of it as a disservice to God who trusted you. Always remember that when you came into the world you came empty handed and when you return after your sojourn on this planet, you go back empty handed. Accept the trust God placed in you when he put you in a position of strength from which you could help or serve others.'

It is a life lesson that has served me in good stead throughout my life.

Chicken Soup in a Brahmin Household!

If I am alive and kicking at 86, it is thanks to the two Gods in my life—my father and my mother. We attribute God-like qualities in humans who are willing to make sacrifices, show love, compassion, understanding and dedicate their efforts tirelessly and selflessly for the well-being of others—be it members of their family or the world at large.

At the age of eleven when we were living in 'Anugraham', the name of our house in Bangalore Cantonment, I developed a rare medical condition called Juvenile Rheumatism. The disease strikes the whole body and every little joint feels as if it has gone dry, making movement very painful. To look after a child in that condition can be very strenuous and testing. My parents, despite having to look after twelve other kids, took extra special care of me. It is thanks to them that I am living today with no pain in my joints.

I was taken to various doctors. Several medicines were prescribed including the expensive chicken essence, which came in glass vials. It was supposed to strengthen bones and muscles, relieve fatigue and was seen as a health tonic. My mother, reconciled to feeding her child with chicken essence, despite being a staunch Brahmin and a strict vegetarian.

On his part, my father narrated my problem to many of his friends and sought their advice. He finally learnt about Vishagarbha Taila, an ayurvedic herbal oil externally applied to treat stiffness of limbs and joints. Those days it was manufactured by Zandu Pharmacy. My father purchased the oil and would ask me to stretch out on a straw mat in our compound. He would then rub the oil on every joint of mine and gently give me a massage It became a ritual every night—I in my shorts lying on the mat and father working on my limbs.

To bolster my health, my mother would prepare several rich and nutritive dishes specially for me. This was fed to me in the kitchen so that it would be out of the gaze of the other children in the house. I can still remember the *gulab jamun* made from urad dal and soaked in sugar syrup that she made exclusively for me.

It was kept in a glass jar in her room. I was to take one piece every morning. But my elder brother Subbu learnt about the special treat kept in mother's room and would follow me each morning. If I ate one gulab jamun, he would secretly swallow two. My mother was naturally worried about my consuming too many gulab jamuns but did not make it an issue.

Meanwhile, as per medical advice I was being given chicken essence in vials which was proving to be expensive. Then someone suggested that we could request our driver Ahmed to make soup at home in our garage. That would certainly cut costs. The idea was discussed at home and finally it was my mother who decided. 'Yes, for my child I will do anything,' she declared. The staunch Brahmin mother reconciled and ignored her Brahmin culture and vegetarian upbringing just for the sake of her son. It was, to my mind, a very bold and noble gesture since I knew how cooking meat was frowned upon in traditional households.

So, Ahmed the driver became a cook every morning. He would bring chicken pieces every morning, boil them with a little bit of salt. He would then filter the clear soup for me while keeping the chicken pieces for himself.

Drinking the soup was literally a ritual. I had to go to the garage with just a thin towel wrapped around my waist and swallow the soup that Ahmed had prepared. Once done I had to come to the threshold of the house where my mother would be waiting with a bucket of warm water which she poured over me to cleanse me of the sin of having drunk the chicken soup. This was a ritual she went through for over six months.

If I am active today without any pain in my joints, I must thank her and my father for having nurtured me through those dark days. The secret of my good health is the dedication my parents showed to save their sick child, even at the cost of sacrificing their staunch religious beliefs. I will always remember them with reverence and respect.

Very Much a Child's Play

In the play *As You like It*, one of Shakespeare's characters famously observed that 'All the world's a stage.' Very true, but as much as we are all actors in our daily lives, I as a child longed to be on the stage entertaining others.

This story goes back to when I was about twelve. Our house in Bangalore had a garage and a huge compound. I was then in the second year of middle school and had a few friends in the immediate neighbourhood. They were all by nature interested in taking part in any activity that provided fun and entertainment.

So, I and my friends got together and planned to put up a variety entertainment show in our garage. We called it *Vividha Vinoda Havali* (A Riot of Variety Entertainment). For two weeks we practiced in our garage and decided to put up the show on a Sunday evening.

We collected about Rs 5 between us and pleaded with a printing press owner in the neighbourhood to oblige us by printing entry tickets of 4 annas each. In all forty tickets were printed, valued at about Rs 10. We sold all forty to our parents and friends and raised Rs 10. Since the cost of printing was Rs 5 we manged to make an equal amount as profit.

We promised ticket holders one hour of entertainment in our garage. Consequently, all who bought tickets, mostly women and children, came to the show. As a backdrop for the stage, we tied together a few bedsheets and my sister Saraswathi and cousin Kamala kicked the show off by singing songs. My mother was happy to see that some activity providing mirth and joy was taking place in our house

By the time the sun set, the *Vividha Vinoda Havali* had to wind up since there were no lights in the garage. But the audience had their share of fun because we made them laugh with our skits and performances. A splendid time was promised, and we kids felt we had delivered.

Soon the audience began to disperse. But as the ladies who attended the show began to leave, my mother looked embarrassed. She suddenly realised that when married ladies came visiting, the hostess was supposed to offer *kumkum* (red turmeric powder), coconuts, betel leaves and seek their blessings. That was the tradition.

My mother immediately rushed the servant to fetch coconuts, betel leaves, and packets of kumkum. She then gave it to the guests who went away happily. After everyone left my mother took me to task, 'Hey, you didn't tell me you were going to call all these ladies. Because of you, I had to spend on coconuts and betel leaves for so many of them.' Of course, I did not breathe a word to her about the profit we made.

Vividha Vinoda Havali ended up being a 'punishment' of sorts for my mother and entertainment for the rest. But within her I don't think she minded it one bit.

A Suitable Sari—My Sister Saraswathi and I

My elder sister Saraswathi and I studied at the Mission Schools near the Corporation office in Bangalore. She was in the London Mission School and I in the United Mission School. Both institutions stood on opposite sides of the road. I was 12 and she was14.

My mother had laid down the rule that I must accompany my sister to school. And Saraswathi, almost as if she did it on purpose, invariably made me wait while she got ready. She would say she was applying kumkum or something to that effect to justify the delay. We used to often quarrel about starting late.

To make matters worse, just as we walked and came towards Langford Town Circle, about half a kilometre from home, we would near the home of Saraswathi's friends—the Devaputra daughters, as they were referred to. They also attended the same school as my sister and as we came close to their house our timing would be in sync with Mr Devaputra dropping his daughters to school in his car. Right on cue they would call out to my sister, and she would gleefully jump into the car and speed away leaving me behind.

Incidentally, I was not allowed in the car since I was a boy! So, I had to walk to school alone and often reached late. At times I had to even run. Much as I complained to my mother she refused to relent. 'No, you have to accompany her. She can't go out alone from the house,' she would say and that was that. So, this became my routine and we used to regularly fight on that account.

Six years later, Saraswathi and I were going to different colleges but on our own. One day I requested her for a sari which I needed for a play I was directing. She wanted to know who was going to wear it. I said my friend who was playing a female part. She refused outright, 'No way,' she said emphatically. 'I won't give my sari to be worn by someone else. If you were to wear it, yes, I would have given it.'

However, she suspected that I might steal one of her saris. So, she put all of them in a box, locked it, and kept the key with her. So, I had no way of getting a sari from her for my play. I knew I had to tap other sources.

So, I went to my older sister Lakshmi who lived with her in-laws. I requested her to help me with a sari. She was agreeable but said she would have to first ask her mother-in-law. Mercifully the latter did not raise any objections. Instead, to my relief she said, 'Certainly, he can have it, I know he acts well. Why, I can give him one of my saris.' Her sari turned out to be suitable since it perfectly fit the character of the elderly lady in the play.

After the play was successfully staged, Saraswathi was very curious and pestered me to tell her how I managed the show without her sari. She wanted to know from where I got one. I was a trifle angry with her and so I retorted, 'You didn't give me your sari. So, how dare you ask me? Let's say I got it from somewhere—why are you so concerned?'

But she continued pestering me. Two days after the play I received the photographs of the performance. In those days we only had black and white photographs. Anyway, I was showing the pictures to my mother when this sister of mine jumped in and said she wanted to have a look. 'Give them to me. I want to see them,' she demanded and had her way.

One look at the photographs and she exclaimed, 'This sari belongs to Lakshmi's mother-in-law!' I couldn't believe it and was quite taken aback by her observation. My mother was amused but not happy that I had approached our *beegarus* (in-laws of a daughter) for a sari. I guess it was a bit unconventional those days.

However, I justified what I had done by pointing out that I had no other option since Saraswathi had refused to part with one of her saris for a day.

Nine Brothers, Four Sisters and Food Supply Management

Since we lived in a house named `Anugraham' we were popularly referred to as the 'Anugraham family'. We were indeed a busy and vibrant household. Other than my parents there were thirteen children (nine brothers and four sisters). Hats off to my father and mother for ensuring that all of us children were well educated and well settled in life.

Among the nine sons, four grew up to become engineers. The others an advocate, a chartered accountant, a doctor, a social scientist, and a journalist. Three of the daughters were graduates and all four were married to engineers.

The credit of educating the thirteen children goes to our parents equally. Father for planning and providing the necessary resources to ensure an education for all, and mother for managing the household with the available resources. The physical endurance of my mother to feed the family of fifteen persons 365 days of the year was mind blowing. Until father was in government service she was assisted by some servants, but the kitchen was run by her.

To ease her work, we boys did a few chores like filling water at 3 a.m. when the water supply was turned on by the municipality, shopping for groceries and vegetables, worshipping before the family deity and serving lunch and dinner for the family. Incidentally, all members, except my father who sat on a chair with a table, squatted on the floor with their plates before them.

When we were growing up, it was not unusual for close friends and relatives to drop in unannounced. Such guests were offered lunch or dinner or both, which they normally accepted. It was then left to mother's ingenuity to somehow manage serving food for all. One method she employed was to restrict the dishes served to the family members without the guest sensing it. Another was to serve and finish the leftovers from the previous meal.

Two ingenious codes, which were only known to family members, were used by those serving food when guests had to be suddenly factored in. Therefore 'CRS', muttered to family members meant that the 'Compulsory Reduction Scheme' had kicked in so no one should ask for a second helping.

The code 'CCS' meant 'Compulsory Consumption Scheme'. It conveyed the message that a particular dish served had to be consumed fully by family members whether they liked it or not. Guests had no such obligation. This was how mother manged the crisis and saw to it that food was distributed so that the family as well as the guests were served, although the latter were given preferential treatment. On such occasions, it was usually a son who used to help mother serve a meal.

In such a large family sibling rivalry was common. Occasions like lunch and dinner were used by the person serving food to embarrass or irritate a sibling with whom he had a grudge. For instance, he would serve a tiny bit or nothing of the item declared CRS, and push in a lot of the CCS items.

Complaints were not entertained by mother. Other members of the family noticed what was going on but chose to remain silent witnesses. The guests, oblivious to the games being played before their own eyes, would quietly enjoy their meal.

We managed thanks to our food supply management skills. Led by mother, we kids ensured that the supply-demand equation was such that the former could meet the latter.

Watching Movies For Free

We all learn valuable lessons in life from our parents. One which remains embedded in my mind till today was something that happened in Chikmagalur when I was fourteen. My father was posted there as the deputy commissioner, and I was occasionally sent to stay with him while the rest of the family remained in Bangalore. The idea was that at least one member of the family was always with him.

Life in Chikmagalur (some 240 kms from Bangalore) was very comfortable and well organised. Whenever I went out of the big bungalow allotted to my father, a policeman would accompany me. Left on my own I was often tempted to go with friends to the local cinema, especially when my father went out of town on tour.

The first time I and my friends went to a cinema theatre, the constable accompanying me went inside and spoke to the manager or the proprietor. Immediately we were all ushered in and seated in the premium balcony section without any of us buying tickets. That was not all, we were served soft drinks because I was after all the deputy commissioner's son.

So that tempted me and my friends to head for the movie theatre every time a new film was released. My buddies would all come and pester me to accompany them to the cinema. All of us were quite enamoured by the idea of catching the first show of a new film.

One day, my father asked me whether I would like to accompany him to a place called Mudigere, about 35 km from Chikmagalur for the inauguration of an event in the evening. Since my friends and I had already planned to go for a film, I lied to my father that I would rather stay at home and study. My father said that was fine by him.

I reckoned that since he left at 3:30 in the afternoon, he would only return by 9.30 p.m. or 10 p.m. By that time, I thought I would be back home from the movies. So, as we had planned, my friends and I went for the evening show and were promptly ushered into the balcony and served our soft drinks.

The picture dragged on and on upsetting my calculations. At about 9:40 p.m. I saw two torches being flashed across the balcony as if someone was searching for somebody in the audience. I discovered to my horror that two constables were looking for me! I asked them what had happened. One of them broke the news: 'Your father has come back, and he is very upset.'

I ran from the theatre like nobody's business, jumped over the compound fence and rushed home. I saw my father pacing up and down while the cook, driver, his assistant, and constables stood by nervously. I knew I was in for trouble.

As soon as I got past the gate my father said with a sigh of relief that I had come back. He told the constables and others that they could leave and asked the cook to go and lay the table for dinner.

He then took me into the bedroom and asked pointedly, 'Where did you go?'

I sheepishly replied that I had gone for a film.

'But you said you wanted to study,' father said angrily.

'Yes, but my friends wanted to go to the pictures, so I went with them.'

'Okay, but where did you get the money for the tickets?' father asked.

'Money? No, they don't take money from the deputy commissioner's son,' I said rather innocently.

The next thing I felt was tight slaps on my cheeks. In fact, father was so furious that he even kicked me, and I fell, but he did not stop. He seemed possessed with anger. Thankfully he regained his composure in a while and then told me to have my dinner. He saw to it that I ate my food that night.

The next morning when I woke up father had left for Bangalore without informing me. He was so upset that he had gone to my mother to share his agony and frustration. I later learnt that he had told her, 'I don't know why this boy has done this. It has really affected my integrity. My self-respect is destroyed by this child. He has gone to the pictures without paying for his ticket because he is the deputy commissioner's son. I don't know what I have done to him in my anger. You please come and take care of him.'

So, my mother came to Chikmagalur the next day. By that time, I was normal and was running around and playing in the compound. But when I saw my parents, I ran back into the bungalow. My mother took me aside and felt every part of my body to ascertain whether there were any broken bones. She then held me close and said, 'What have you done. You should be careful about these things. How are you? Are you alright?'

Even as she poured her affection, she explained to me the wrong I had done. 'Do you realise you have harmed your father's image? He is the head of the district and cannot afford to have his son or any of his family members behave in a manner which questions his integrity and reputation. We all should be very careful and not do anything that hurts his image.'

I learnt my first lesson in integrity that day. It has remained with me till today.

The Chikmagalur Conspiracy

Since my childhood I was fascinated by theatre. There was something about the stage and everything associated with it that fuelled my imagination and passion. I looked forward to every opportunity to act and the staging of a play was always an event not to be missed.

In the early 1950s whenever I stayed with my father in Chikmagalur and he went away on official tours, I would seize the opportunity to ask for a role in the play that the local theatre group—'Kalaseva Sanga'— was then practicing.

I remember landing a role in *Chakravyuh* in which I was given the part of the son of a very honest government official who was troubled and tortured by some devious persons because he refused the bribes offered to him. Finally, unable to bear the pressure from his boss to compromise his values, he dies.

His son, the role which I was given, cries inconsolably, and with that the play ends. I used to perform the crying scene rather well and made many in the audience cry with me. I thoroughly enjoyed playing that part.

On one of my later visits to Chikmagalur, the Kalaseva Sanga decided to stage the play again and they urged me to perform the crying scene. But I had a problem. My SSLC exam was just twenty days away and I was staying with my father so that I could study in peace in the big bungalow without any interference from my brothers and sisters.

So, I asked the folks from the theatre group to first seek my father's permission before I could take part in the play. Most of those in the Kalaseva Sanga were either clerks or junior officials in the district or taluk office. They were naturally hesitant to approach the deputy commissioner to request his son's participation in a play. However, some of them did have a word with my father. He said he was happy to learn that they thought so highly of my acting skills, but he said he could not give me permission. 'My son has an important examination coming up shortly, so you will have to excuse him this time. After his exams are over, I will have no objection,' he said.

When I later met them, they looked dejected since they could not have me perform the grand finale of the play. They said they would have to train somebody else for the role.

Within me I was very keen and determined to be on the stage since I loved the part so much. In those days, dramas were staged late night between 10 p.m. and 2 a.m. One part of me said I must participate in the play, but the other half wanted me to resign myself to the fact that I could not since I had a crucial exam coming up.

My mother was also in Chikmagalur to be with me ahead of the SSLC exam. So, I was left with no option but to stay at home and study. In any case, I could not have possibly attended any of the rehearsals with my mother supervising my studies.

On the day the play was being staged I sat in my room in the bungalow with my books. But all the while I was planning on how I could be on stage despite my mother keeping a watch on me. And then an idea came to my mind.

That night I conspired with the police constable on duty. I explained my dilemma to him. He understood my plight. Moreover, he was a fan of mine since he had seen my performance when the play was staged earlier. So, I took him into confidence and made him a co-conspirator in my plan.

I told him that I would leave the light on in my room and bolt the door from the inside and pretend to study. I would however exit from the other door. This was where he would come in. 'You will have to keep the light on till 9 p.m. and then switch it off. If mother comes and asks, you must say that I was studying and had slept off.'

As planned, I scooted from the bungalow and ran to the theatre where the play was scheduled to be performed. Another boy, my substitute, was in the green room getting ready. I kicked up a shindy. 'Nothing doing, nobody else will play my role.' I said at the top of my voice. This ruckus, just when the audience was filing in, upset the organisers no end. Incidentally, they were not very happy with the substitute boy's performance, so, they gave in to my pleas.

That evening, moved by my acting, many women in the audience shed tears. In those days the practice was to throw money on to the stage if one was impressed by an actor's acting, I daresay my talent did encourage the audience to loosen their purse strings.

While I was pleased with the response I got, I was also worried about getting back home before my absence was detected.

So, I rushed home as soon as the play was over and met the constable. When I asked him if my mother had enquired about me, he said 'Amma had come after I put off the light in your room. I told her you were reading, but had just slept, then she went away.'

Greatly relieved, I washed my face and scrubbed it till there was no trace of any makeup and went back to bed. The next morning, I played totally innocent and ate my breakfast as usual.

Soon my exams were over, and I was back in Bangalore. But after I left Chikmagalur a sequence of events happened which almost exposed my little caper on the night of the play. Here is a reconstruction of what transpired:

On the day after I left Chikmagalur, my mother fell ill. The deputy commissioner's wife getting sick shook up the medical administration in the district which immediately deputed Kalavathy, a nurse, to take care of mother.

While chatting Kalavathy casually mentioned my acting skills. 'Amma your son is such a wonderful actor. He made us all cry the other day.' My mother was intrigued. 'What do you mean? In which play did you see him?'

She said she had seen me in *Chakravyuh* which was staged three weeks before. 'Lot of us in the audience really cried. The way your son acted was wonderful and very touching. People were saying that the boy playing the role was the deputy commissioner's son Padmanabha.'

My mother protested, 'No, you are mistaken. He could not have been there on the stage. I know he wanted to play the role, but he was not allowed to. He was here at home studying that night.'

But Kalavathy was emphatic in her response, 'No madam, I am sure he was on the stage. In fact, I can get some of my colleagues from the hospital to confirm it since they were also there that night. They all said the boy was the deputy commissioner's son.'

So, my mother wrote me an angry letter in which she recounted what Kalavathy had told her and admonished me for having cheated her and father. I wrote back to her saying 'You have more faith in a nurse than your own son. I wanted to act that day, but I never did. I was very disappointed and now I get this letter from you.' She responded with a very apologetic letter in which she wrote, 'I am sorry. I think I should have believed you, not the nurse.'

Her apology was painful to absorb and increased my guilt many times over. In fact, it lingered on for a long time and reminded me of my dishonesty towards my mother. Even after twenty-five years it continued to prick my conscience. So, on one occasion when I came to Bangalore on a visit, I went straight to mother and prostrated myself before her and confessed. 'I told you a lie but please pardon me. I did cheat you on that day.'

By then I had grown up with two children of my own. Mother laughed and asked me details of how I managed to slip out of the house. 'I knew you were very involved with the play, but I never thought that you could manage things that way,' she said.

Luckily for me no one had breathed a word about it to my father. And my mother did not share with him what the nurse had told her because she was protective towards her son. She had probably also waited for a clarification from my side.

Tracking a Dead Soul

Looking back, it is easy to see the funny side of incidents that deeply embarrassed you when they happened. In fact, recounting stories from the past with humour thrown in could even prove to be entertaining for the narrator as well as the reader or listener. But deep within, you know that some of these incidents made you introspect and taught you a lesson or two that remains with you throughout your life.

Here is a story that illustrates the point I am making. I was about eighteen or nineteen and at that point in life when I thought and breathed theatre as if nothing else mattered. I would forget everything else, however important, because I felt theatre was my top priority. But an incident taught me that one can't be so oblivious as to be irresponsible and disregard the sentiments of others.

My drama in real life began with my mother —whom we called 'Akka'—wanting to perform *Hoovillya*, a ritual in which the lady of the house invited a few married women home and gifted them goodies and sought their *aashirvaada* (blessings). My mother had fixed the ceremony for a Saturday.

We were living in Langford Town and my mother asked me on a Wednesday of the week before the event to meet Subbamma on my way to college and ask her to come home the following Wednesday to prepare the goodies. Now, Subbamma was a familiar figure in our household. She had been coming to our house for well over a decade to help mother in the kitchen on special occasions.

I assured my mother that I would run the errand for her. But by evening I forgot all about it since I got caught up in a rehearsal of a play. It was only at ten in the night that I remembered that I had not met Subbamma. I rushed to the shop in Basavanagudi's Gandhi Bazar, near my college, which she ran. It had closed for the day.

When I reached home, my mother was waiting for me. 'Did you manage to meet Subbamma?' she asked. I said I had got late and would certainly meet her the following day. The next two days saw a repeat of what had already happened: I went to college, got caught up in the rehearsals and by the time I remembered I found the shop had closed.

By Sunday mother was a little worried. But I reassured her that I would contact Subbamma on Monday. But alas, I forgot once again.

Finding the shop closed I did not know what to tell my mother. In fact, not knowing how to face her, I thought I had no option but to lie to her that I had contacted Subbamma and she had agreed to come home on Thursday. Mother was very relieved when she heard the news.

Before I went to bed, I told myself that I must make it a point to contact Subbamma the following morning at her home and persuade her to accept the assignment. If I waited for the rehearsals to be over in the evening, I might miss her again.

Early next morning before Akka got up, I took the cycle and rushed to Subbamma's shop. It was closed. But in the vicinity some women were selling flowers and pooja materials. I asked one of them when the shop would open. The woman said around 9:30 a.m. and then wondered why I was enquiring? I said I wanted to go to Subbamma's house. The woman promptly gave me directions.

I was happy that things had gone well thus far and proceeded to Subbamma's house and knocked at the door. 'Who is that?' a female voice enquired as the door opened. A young woman stood in front of me wondering who I was.

'I have come from the cantonment area. I am Parvathamma's son. I want to speak to Subbamma.' I said introducing myself.

'Subbamma!' She exclaimed, 'Don't you know she died six months ago?'

I was stunned. It felt as if the whole world had collapsed on me. I did not know what to say. So, I took my cycle and headed back home dumbfounded. On the way, my mind was working overtime on how I would convey this shocking news to mother.

When I reached home the first thing mother asked me was 'I hope Subbamma is coming?' I sheepishly broke the news that she would not be able to come.

Pat came the next question: 'What do you mean she can't come?'

I prostrated myself at mother's feet begging forgiveness.

'Why what happened? What is it? Has she been engaged elsewhere?'

I said I would tell her if she promised to forgive me. Mother assured me that she would pardon me. So, I blurted out, 'Subbamma can't come because she is no more.'

To my utter surprise, mother burst out laughing. I had never seen her laugh so loudly and so uncontrollably. I was shocked at her inexplicable response. Finally, she said, 'This is what happens when you tell a lie to your mother. Hereafter, don't tell lies.'

Her next anxiety filled question was what she would do about the function on Saturday. 'How am I going manage the event?' she wondered aloud. I promised her that I would find somebody else.

That day my priority changed to Akka's *Hoovillya* and I found someone who would come and help. The event, mercifully, went off well. And I learnt an unforgettable lesson.

III
From the College Years

How Father Opened My Eyes

If I recall right, the year was 1958. I had already failed twice in my BSc and 'Anna', as I called my father, was very concerned about where I was heading in life. Most of the time I was involved in amateur theatre, and I would drop everything else if I had to go and rehearse a play.

In fact, so worried was my father that one day he took me to the stone benches placed in one quiet corner of the compound of our house. He made me sit down and said he wished to speak to me for a few minutes. He then said after a long pause, 'Yesterday I was travelling to Mysore on work by train in the first-class compartment where I happened to meet the famous Tamil actor, Manohar. He was my fellow passenger.'

My father went on to say that when he learnt he was in the company of a film star, he poured out his concern for me, his son, who was totally immersed in theatre and acting. He sought Manohar's advice. 'I don't know where my son is heading. Do you think this boy can make a living out of this kind of activity?' he had asked.

Manohar apparently asked him several questions about what I was doing, how many times I had failed in college and my passion for theatre. Manohar finally told him not to worry, 'Sir, you don't worry about your boy. He will make it big as an actor. The way you are describing your son, he seems totally involved in acting. He will succeed.' With that he gave father his visiting card with his address in Madras and told him, 'Please send him to me. He can stay in my house, and I will groom him. You don't have to worry after that. From all that you have told me I think we have a young, dedicated actor whom I would like to help.'

So, after he narrated his chance encounter with Manohar, father gave me the actor's card and said 'Look, I have tried my best to emphasize the importance of education. You don't seem to agree. Now you can do one thing—I will give you the money. You go to Madras, meet this gentleman, and see if you can take up acting as a profession. This is what I can do, and I wish you all the best.'

I was totally stunned by my father's advice since it came from a man who was traditional and did not think much of the film industry. It struck me very hard that he was going against his values and making compromises for a son. So, I said, 'Anna, give me two days to think about it.'

For the next two days I spent much time on the terrace introspecting. I kept asking myself the question: 'What do I want in life? Do I want to be an actor and make a living out of it?' Those days in Chikmagalur and other places where I used to act with several professional troupes, it was the common practice for the audience to throw money on the stage whenever somebody acted well and that was what the actors of the troupe earned. They were at the mercy of the audience.

I had also seen the life actors lived. They stayed in small poorly appointed houses. In the evening they would laze around in their costumes, and with makeup on their faces they looked bright and colourful. But otherwise, they lived miserable lives. I questioned myself: 'Do I want to collect money on the stage and eke out an existence?' That led me to the next question: 'Why do I want to act?' Finally, the answer came very clearly to me— I wanted to act for my enjoyment.

That realization made things clear to me. As far as acting was concerned, it was an activity that I enjoyed so I must pursue it as a hobby. But I would have to find something else to do to earn a living. On the evening of my second day of introspection, I arrived at the conclusion that to make a good living I needed an education. So, I resolved that hereafter I would concentrate on my studies. As far as theatre was concerned, I would spare free time towards it but not at the cost of my education.

I went to my father as I promised and gave back Manohar's card. I said, 'Anna, your concern for me has made me think and introspect. Thank you very much for that. Henceforth you will not have to worry about how I fare in my examinations or my studies. I am very disturbed that I have caused you so much pain.'

He was obviously relieved. 'No, no it was no pain. It is a pleasure to hear you say that you will be committed to your studies. God bless you.'

That was it. From then on theatre became my hobby. That year I completed my BSc. and went on to study law. Later I enrolled at the Tata Institute of Social Sciences, Bombay for a postgraduate course in social science.

Even though I had consciously downgraded theatre from my singular passion to a hobby, there were colourful memories from my acting days in National College that I still cherish. Some of them can still bring a smile. Here is one such hilarious incident.

I had two friends from college who shared my passion for theatre. One was B.N. Nani alias Makeup Nani whom I called 'Guru.' The other was B.R. Jayaram. We were very thick, and fun loving and enjoyed pulling each other's legs even while on stage.

In 1958 we put up the play *Ajji Aasthi'* (Grandmother's Treasure) in which I was the Ajji (grandmother) and Jayaram and Nani played her grandsons. The storyline was straightforward. The aged Ajji had a piece of cloth in which she had tied up something and carried the bundle very carefully with her. At night she slept with it under her head and never allowed anyone to even touch it. So, the grandsons assumed that Ajji had hidden money or gold in the bundle.

On the day the play was being staged, Nani, Jayaram and I had a difference of opinion on some issue. So, we got into an argument in the makeup room. Nani and Jayaram were a bit upset, so they said that since I was arrogant, they would teach me a lesson on stage.

In the play, Ajji was to be fed some medicine twice by her grandsons, after which she dies. To teach me a lesson, what Nani and Jayaram did was to fill the 'medicine' bottle with water mixed with colour from the makeup room. On stage, when they were to feed medicine to Ajji, they made me drink the dirty concoction while whispering to me that I was paying for behaving arrogantly and arguing with them. I had to somehow gulp the dirty water down.

To make matters worse, the script demanded that Ajji would not die with the first dose of medicine and would be fed a second one by her grandsons. So, Nani and Jayaram playing the evil grandsons came on stage and fed me another dose of the dirty water. This time they held my nose to make sure I drank it.

After the second dose Ajji was to die. But I decided to take revenge against Naani and Jayaram and refused to pass away! So Ajji had to be given a third and fourth dose, but she still refused to die. Nani and Jayaram didn't know what to do because they had to deliver their dialogues which were written for the scene after Ajji was dead. Now they would have to improvise which was a tough call.

The prompter, Seetharam, went blank at the strange turn of events. So, Nani exited the stage saying that he would return only after Ajji really died. He then directed the prompter to take corrective action, 'Hey go, hold Ajji by the neck and see that she doesn't get up again,' he was told. So Seetharam moved from the wings to behind the stage and pushed his hand from under the backdrop to where I was lying on a cot and held my neck and threatened to kill me if I did not give up my ghost. So Ajji died ultimately!

The audience was roaring with laughter as they watched Jayaram pathetically trying to blabber some made up dialogue. Meanwhile a gentleman in the audience, sensing a problem, shouted 'When are you closing this play?'

That was one of our many antics on stage. We used to enjoy playing such pranks.

One other incident that still brings a smile involved B.R. Jayaram who was an excellent actor and very innovative on stage. He would spontaneously deviate from dialogues in the script to evoke laughter among the audience. Those acting with him played along till he got back to the theme of the play.

Depending on the audience and its mood, Jayaram would come out with new lines which would add spice to the story. He would do this regularly and some of us on the stage with him would also try to match him, to enrich the overall dramatic effect.

Once, while practicing for a play, a newcomer was inducted to play a small role. Jayaram playing the lead went off the script and improvised. The newcomer looked flabbergasted with a blank expression on his face. He was lost not knowing how to respond to Jayaram's improvised dialogue.

I explained to the newcomer, 'Look, Jayaram is like this, sometimes he strays from the script. You don't have to respond. Watch him quietly, he will soon get back to the original dialogue.'

We all knew that Jayaram loved to play such pranks and knew how to handle him. But why did he have to try it with a newcomer? So, I told him, 'Jayaram, you do it with me or Seetharam. We know how to adjust but don't do it with newcomers. It makes them nervous.'

His response was quick: 'How else do I make them learn? You don't worry. They will all get used to it.'

I was a trifle irritated with his attitude so I said, 'Okay then, I will also catch you unaware to teach you a lesson.'

I got my chance at the annual festival held on the bed of the Kempambhudi Kere lake in Bangalore when the water body died up in summer. That was when the Municipal Corporation organised a festival there which attracted quite a crowd. Incidentally, the lake is no more since it was later dried and levelled and today houses the Kempegowda bus stand.

One particular year the organisers invited the Histrionics Club of National College, where we were all students, to put up a play. We decided to stage *Alia Devaru* (Sons-in-Law) in which my role was that of a theatre actor and Jayaram played the part of a homeopathy doctor. When the play began, I was on the stage and Jayaram made his entry blabbering the dialogue. 'Oh, I am so busy, I have no time even to scratch myself.'

Since I had promised to pull his leg, I thought this was an opportune moment to give Jayaram a taste of his own medicine. So, I improvised. 'You call yourself a busy homeopathy doctor. Do you at least know how the word homeopathy was coined?'

He was taken aback by my strange question, but he composed himself in a few seconds, and replied, 'Oh that word, it is a long story, you wait, and I will tell you.'

Then he began moving around the stage, first taking off his tie. Then he removed his coat, went to the back of the stage to hang it, took off the hat and went to the other corner of the stage to keep it. He then picked up his doctor's bag to keep it on a stool in one corner. He kept the attention of the audience focused on his movements without uttering a word.

I could see that his mind was concocting the story he would tell to explain the origin of the word homeopathy. He then suddenly asked me to sit on a chair and listen to his story while he seated himself across me.

His fabricated story ran something like this: 'In ancient India there was a famous writer called Shake Peer. He had a daughter named Homeo. Her husband suffered from a rare disease which caused rashes all over his body, for which local doctors found a medicine. It was prepared by collecting cow's urine in the morning and adding bee wax, horse dung and donkey's milk to it.' The audience kept roaring with laughter without knowing that Jayaram was spinning out an impromptu dialogue.

Meanwhile, I kept whispering to him, 'Jaya please stop it, I am sorry for pulling your leg" to which he whispered back 'You pulled my leg, so you now pay for it.'

Luckily, to my great relief after a few more minutes he pulled the play back to the original script. I realized that improvisation on stage was a rare talent that Jayaram possessed. The good thing was that the audience simply loved his antics on stage.

Jayaram and I are still great friends.

Hard Work Does Not Always Pay

We have always been told that if you put in sustained effort, you will reap the reward. There is indeed a lot of truth in that saying. But sometimes luck can shine on the not so hardworking who may outpace those who have put in an effort. Nowhere is this true as in examinations where a student better known for bunking classes might fare better than those who attended every lecture and religiously took notes.

This can happen because in the build up to the examination the student who missed his classes might simply study key portions from where all the questions are framed, or he may have consulted a senior student who explained critical portions to him. It is all a matter of luck.

While I was in my final year BSc at Vijaya College, I was irregular in classes, including the Kannada lectures. One day when I did not have any theatre activity, I attended the Kannada class, which was a combined one for both male and female students. The teacher was a was a gentleman held in high esteem as a profoundly knowledgeable person in Kannada literature.

While he was writing something on the board, a mischievous backbencher made a paper plane and floated it towards the girls seated in front. The teacher. turning back from the board, noticed the plane landing. He became very angry and not knowing who was responsible for the mischief concluded that it must have been me since I was attending his class after many days.

In a stern admonishing voice, he turned to me and said, 'Padmanabha, I don't care whether you attend my class or not, but when you come don't wag your tail before me.' The whole class went silent. Since I had done nothing wrong, I stood up and in an equally stern voice responded, 'Sir, firstly I did not throw that paper plane. You are mistaken. And then, I cannot accept the expression "don't wag your tail" that you used. Aren't you aware that we are grown up boys and using such expressions in a combined class is humiliating? Hereafter I am not attending your classes.' With that I walked out.

The matter was taken up with the principal, who had his own scores to settle with the Kannada teacher. So, he found it convenient to let the matter lie unresolved. In any case, those days we could pay a fine for attendance shortage and get away with it. So, my boycott of the Kannada class did not stop me from attending the exam.

But while preparing for the Kannada paper a day before the exam I realized that I had not so much as touched one of the prescribed texts—*Kanooru Subbamma Heggadihti* by Kannada writer Kuvempu.

Not knowing what to do at the last minute, I rang up my friend Ramu who lived in Jayanagar. I asked him if was revising the novel in question. When he answered in the affirmative, I asked him if I could join him while he went over the book. Reluctantly he agreed. So, I went to his house around 8 p.m. and kept listening to him reading the chapter summaries till 4 a.m.

Then I returned home and was in the college at 8 a.m. for the exam. When I came out of the exam hall, I bumped into the Kannada teacher who told me to offer 'tarpana' (offerings to the gods) and hope for the best.

When the results were announced, I had passed in Kannada, but poor Ramu had failed!

A similar situation arose in my first-year law exam. As usual, I had not prepared well for it. But I was friends with G.S. Vishweswara, a student one year my senior. Just before the exam I realized that I had totally neglected a section—the 'Transfer of Property Act'—which carried 100 marks. The prescribed text book not only ran into several hundred pages, but its language was also rather unfamiliar to me.

Understanding the gravity of the situation, I made a beeline for Vishweswara's room and begged him to help me. Predictably, he took me to task for my carelessness, but agreed to teach me. From around 7 p.m, till 5 a.m. he explained things, brushing through each chapter and summarizing the important aspects of the law. At 5 a.m. I returned home and attended the exam three hours later. A month later when the results were announced, I had passed my first year Law.

I went with my marksheet to thank my friend. Seeing it, he was furious and declared that the person who valued my papers was incompetent. When I asked him what he meant he said that the previous year when he wrote the first-year exam, he had scored only 68 per cent, while a useless guy like me whom he had given a crash tuition to had scored 73 per cent!

Now, don't get me wrong. I was simply lucky. And, yes, hard work pays.

God Works in Mysterious Ways

I would call this an experience which made me realize that when you appeal sincerely to God, even at the smallest and most unknown of temples, it works. To illustrate this, I must take you back to 1959 when my brother Venu got engaged to his future wife, Jayalakshmi. She and I were to appear for the BSc final exam from Vijaya College.

It was my third attempt. My mother or Akka, as we called her, was very worried that if I failed and Jayalakshmi passed it would be a big embarrassment. At the time of my brother's marriage everybody would be talking about my failure and contrasting it with my sister-in-law's success.

Jayalakshmi was confident that she had already passed, and she told me as much. But I still had my mathematics exam coming up. It was a subject I was weak in. In the first and second maths papers I had not done well despite taking the help of Mr B.M. Srinivasa Rao, my maths tutor. He had tried to impress on me that if I followed logical steps mathematics was easy.

But such logic somehow eluded me. So, I thought the best way out was mugging up theorems and hoping that if I get a few of them in my exams I could scrape through. Mr Rao tried in vain to dissuade me from taking this approach. He suggested I concentrate on astronomy, a subject he liked, which was also part of the third paper in mathematics. But I ignored his advice.

Since I had not fared well in the first two papers, the third paper became crucial. I was all nerves as I cycled from Langford Town to Vijaya College in Jayanagar to attend the exam. As I was passing through the Minerva Talkies area, I saw a temple which I had never visited. So, I instinctively stopped. When I went in, I noticed it was a Hanuman, Sitarama and Eswara temple.

Almost in desperation I prostrated before the gods and pleaded, 'God please help me today. My mother will be terribly embarrassed if I fail, and I don't want to be the cause for it. Please help me.' It was a fervent plea and I hoped that the Gods would listen.

In the exam hall I saw Prof. B.V. Narayana Rao, who always thought of me as a frivolous student who neglected his studies and used to talk rather derisively to me. He was the invigilator.

As soon as the examination got underway, and I went through the question paper all my hopes sank. I was horrified to see that calculus and trigonometry theorems did not figure among the questions. Instead, there were many questions on astronomy which I did not understand. So, at the half-an-hour bell, I got up, ready to leave. Prof. Narayana Rao came up to me and asked me why I had given up. 'Sir there is no question in this paper that I can even attempt. So, I am leaving,' I said.

On hearing this he put his hand on my shoulder and asked, 'Look, what will you be doing if you go out now?' I said maybe I would go and spend time with some friends since I saw no point in sitting in the exam hall when I was in no position to answer any of the questions.

Prof. Rao looked at me and gave me some advice which is till today imprinted in my mind. 'Listen, just sit down, concentrate on the questions, and see whether you can answer them. By going out now and wasting two-and-half hours with friends may not do you any good in life. Instead sit here, concentrate, spend that time finding answers to the questions.'

I was quite taken aback because I never expected the professor would show so much concern for me. I took his advice seriously, sat down, and looked again at the astronomy questions. For some reason, for which I can't offer any explanation, each of the questions suddenly seemed solvable if I used my power of reasoning.

One by one I answered the six questions. I thought I had them right but was not sure. When the time was up Prof. Narayana Rao came up and causally enquired, 'How many supplementary answer sheets did you use?' I said I had taken three of them. He then added 'See those two-and-half hours seems to have done something for you today. God bless you.' I thanked him for the timely advice he had given me.

I ran to Mr Srinivasa Rao my tuition teacher. He said he had asked me to concentrate on astronomy from where all the questions had come. I said 'Sir, I just want to explain how I answered the questions on astronomy.' After he heard me out, he was surprised. 'Yes, you are right. But how did you manage it?' I said, 'I don't know, but I did it.'.

When the results were announced, I had passed. Even today I feel so elated when I remember how happy my mother was when she learnt that I had passed. My prayers had indeed helped. My saviour came in the form of Professor Rao, a gentleman who till that day had never had a kind word for me. I still do not know what made him persuade me not to give up.

God, they say, works in mysterious ways.

Friends, Marriages, Acting and Rum Reflections

The first marriage of a friend where I had a role to play was the wedding of my mentor in theatre, B.B. Nani alias Makeup Nani. I was instrumental in introducing Nani to his future wife Bhargavi. But at that time, I had no clue of the romance that would blossom later. Suffice to say that the two got married and I had inadvertently played Cupid.

Since theatre was Nani's passion it was almost inevitable that he would find his life partner on stage, or as it was in his case, backstage. It was possibly in 1958 that the girls of Vijaya College successfully persuaded the then principal, the late Mr V.T. Srinivasan, to permit them to stage a play. Bhargavi led this initiative. The principal agreed but on one condition—that the performance would be an all-girls one with even the male roles enacted by females.

Jubilant, the girls picked the play *Home Rule* which had four male characters. Consequently, the girls playing those roles needed special makeup to look like men. In those days, there were no makeup artists readily available in Bangalore. And Nani was literally accredited for his skills in this department as his alias 'Makeup' suggested. The principal was persuaded to permit Nani to help but with a strict direction that whatever had to be done would be done in the presence of a lady teacher.

That was when Nani and Bhargavi got introduced. Their friendship began with what I call a professional touch. Later, when Nani had to shift from his uncle's place, and was looking for a room to stay in Bangalore I came into the picture. I happened to be very close to Bhargavi's brother Chintamani and knew that a room had fallen vacant at her house I requested her mother to rent it out to Nani. Though she was initially hesitant to give it to a bachelor since she had an unmarried daughter, she agreed, thanks to my persuasion.

A few months later the inevitable happened and Nani sought Bhargavi's hand in marriage and her mother gave her consent. But her brother Chintamani was furious with me for persuading his mother to have Nani as their tenant. But he reconciled later after the marriage was fixed.

As Nani's friends some of us decided that the marriage would be arranged by us and invitees from both the bride and bridegroom's sides would be our guests. Accordingly, we made all the arrangements, and the marriage was held at the Ramakrishna Students Hostel.

Later, at the reception, I was among those serving dinner. A few well-known journalists seated to partake the food suddenly whispered in my ear 'Where is the *Gundu*', meaning something alcoholic to drink. Sensing that they would be disappointed without liquor being served, I went to the kitchen and emptied three bottles of rum into a serving vessel, brought a few empty glasses and served it with a ladle.

To mask the fact that I was serving liquor I announced that I was serving *Tili Saaru,* a soup-like traditional preparation brownish in colour. Once I had served the guests from the press, the priests seated opposite them demanded they too be served *Tili Saaru.* Obviously, they had no inkling that it was rum that I was serving. Anyway, caught on the wrong foot I declared that there was no more *Tilli Saaru* to serve and disappeared from the scene!

This real-life story is about G. K. Govinda Rao, another friend from the theatre. In 1957 selections were being held to represent Mysore University at the All India Inter University Youth Festival. It was at the selection stage that Govinda Rao met Manjula. She was part of a drama troupe.

The two fell in love. Govinda Rao was from Central College and belonged to the Madhwa community from Bangalore. Manjula was also from the same community, but from Dharwar. Strangely enough, though from the same community, families from the two regions followed different traditions.

When they decided to get married in 1960, Govinda Rao's family rejected the proposal outright and barred every member of the family from attending the marriage at Hubli. So, when the downcast bridegroom deserted by his family requested me to accompany him to the wedding, I consented.

It proved to be an embarrassing experience. I had to respond to questions from the bride's side relating to wedding procedures which were Greek to me. I somehow mumbled my way through with great difficulty using my skills at improvisation! I was relieved when the ceremony was over. Was I happy to be back home after playing the role of the lone escort of the bridegroom!

There was yet another occasion when I had to use my acting skills to be the best man at a wedding. This time it was at the marriage of Dr Ramachandran, who was my professor at the Tata Institute of Social Sciences (TISS). He later became my professional mentor and a close family friend.

He had fallen in love with his secretary Margaret, a catholic. When the couple decided to tie the knot, Dr Ramachandran's family—staunch Brahmins from Kerala—vehemently opposed the marriage. It was decided by his parents that no family member would attend the wedding at a church in Bandra, Bombay.

So, I became the groom's best man even though I was totally ignorant about catholic weddings. All I did was to dress in a suit and accompany Dr Ramachandran to the altar. There I just followed the instructions of the pastor without an inkling of what I was doing. I recall I was moving like a zombie trying hard to avoid making mistakes!

I discovered that being the best man comes with its share of acting!

IV
The Learning Curve

TISS and Tell

How I manged to get admission into the prestigious Tata Institute of Social Sciences, Bombay, was a story by itself. Without a clue as to what to do after BSc. I was goaded by my father and my brother Shivaram, both lawyers, to study law. So, I joined the Government Law College, Bangalore in 1959 and graduated in 1961.

Since classes were from 7.30 to 10:30 in the morning, it left the afternoons free. My brother found in me a good assistant to have around him in court to run errands for him and father. They would make me fetch documents, contact fellow advocates to obtain an adjournment in another court or entertain clients in the court premises while they waited for the judge to call their case.

I noticed the clients spent much of their time gossiping about something or the other while sipping small cups of coffee. They had taken it as their lot to play the waiting game and sat patiently for hours in the court complex. Many would return to follow the same routine at the next hearing.

I thought my life, despite being hectic, was quite as dull as theirs. On a typical day I would return home in the evening after a day in the court and get busy finding the documents needed for cases listed the next day. I also had to talk to the clients about upcoming hearings.

Frankly, I didn't see much of life in the work I was doing. I felt that the lawyer's profession was not meant for someone like me. But I did not know what else to do. Since I had graduated in law, the world expected me to be a lawyer. But the thought of running from one courtroom to the other for the rest of my life did not particularly enthuse me.

Luckily my destiny changed one morning when I went to a restaurant to have a cup of coffee and ran into my classmate from law school, D.H. Guru. He was the son of the former education minister of Karnataka. Our conversation went something like this:

Me: Hey, what are you doing? Are you practicing?

Guru: No, I decided I don't wish to practice.

Me: Then what are your plans? What do you propose to do?

Guru: I am going to the Tata Institute of Social Sciences or TISS in Bombay.

Me: What happens at this institute?

Guru: They train you in personnel management etc., etc.

Me; Do you have any details about the course you will be joining?"

Guru: I have the syllabus with me. I have got the books prescribed for the course at home.

Me: Can I come and have a look?

Guru: You are most welcome. But I think that the last day for filing applications for this year's course is three days from now. So, you will have to decide quickly.

I went to his house, went through the syllabus, and was totally fascinated by the course. I rushed back home very excited. I was very clear in my mind that I wanted to go to Bombay and join TISS with Guru.

Fortunately, that day my parents were discussing on how to send Kitty, my six-year-old nephew to Bombay. The child's parents— my sister Lakshmi and her husband Anantharamiah— had moved to Bombay but Kitty had to stay behind in Bangalore to complete his school year. My parents were looking for an escort to accompany the child to Bombay.

I saw this as a god sent opportunity to try my luck at TISS. So, I went to my father with the TISS syllabus seeking permission to escort Kitty to Bombay and explore the possibility of joining the institute. My father was obviously puzzled and asked, 'How can you hope to get admission in TISS with your poor academic record? This TISS is a very reputed institute. and this is a postgraduate course.'

I said I knew it was not easy to get admission, but I could at least try. I offered to escort Kitty to Bombay, leave him with his parents and go to the institute and fill in the application form.

He consented to my request perhaps realizing the lack of interest I was showing in court work. At that point my father had a visitor with whom he went outside for a quiet chat in the corner of the compound outside our house where we had stone benches.

I was asked to fetch a cup of coffee for the guest. The gentleman who had come to meet father was Mr Mirza, a friend of his. He was a very well-known advocate in Bangalore and an industrialist. When I went and gave Mr Mirza his coffee he causally enquired as to what I was doing.

I said I was doing nothing at present. 'I have completed my law and I am planning to go to the Tata Institute of Social Sciences in Bombay,' I added.

'The Tata Institute? Oh, its director, Wadia happens to be my cousin. When are you going?'

I said I was taking the train that very day. 'You do one thing' he said, 'after I talk to your dad I will be going home. I will write a note to Wadia. You take it with you. It may be of help.'

I was delighted. This surely was God's intervention, I thought.

Anyway, that afternoon I went and picked up Mr Mirza's note and was on the train to Bombay with Kitty. Once we reached, I lost no time in going to TISS, filling my application form, and submitting it.

The next morning, armed with Mr Mirza's letter, I went to meet Dr Wadia, director of TISS, at his residence. I had learnt that everyone on the campus feared him because he was very strict. When I knocked, he opened the door and asked me what I wanted.

I was nervous but I managed to request him to give me a minute of his time.

'Come in and sit down. What do you want?' He asked again.

'Sir, I have come from Bangalore, and I have applied for admission at your institute. I have a letter from Mr Mirza who asked me to meet you personally and hand it over.'

He read Mr. Mirza's note and then said, 'Okay, you have applied, right? I cannot assure you a seat, but I will see to it that you are called for an interview. You need to clear it, otherwise, I cannot help you.' I thanked him and left.

I returned to Bangalore. About a month later Guru rang me up. 'Padmanabha I have got an interview call from TISS, I am going day after tomorrow.' He added that three days from then was the last day for interviews.

'I haven't got any intimation as yet—no call,' I told him sounding concerned.

'Then perhaps they won't be interviewing you.'

I mulled over what he said and then hesitatingly I went to my father. 'Anna I must go to Bombay. The last day of the interview is three days from now. I want to be there.'

'But you haven't been called for the interview. What can you achieve by going to Bombay?' he asked.

'Dr Wadia said he would call me for the interview. I will meet him and get my name on the list of candidates to be interviewed,' I said with desperation in my voice.

My dad was sympathetic and said I could go and try my luck.

On reaching Bombay I went straight to Dr Wadia's house in the morning. He opened the door. 'Sir, I had come to you with Mr Mirza's letter. You had told me that I would be called for an interview. I thought I would at least get a fair opportunity to prove myself, but I have not got an interview call,' I reminded him.

'Okay, yes, I remember your coming. Now go and meet my personal assistant, Mr Iyer. I will phone him and tell him to include you in the interview list. Today is the last day for interviews.'

I rushed to his office. By that time Guru's interview was over. When I met Mr Iyer, he informed me that my interview was the last one for the day and was slotted for 5 p.m.

When my turn came, I walked into a room where a group of professors on the panel were waiting. The interview began with the usual formalities and pleasantries.

Then a member of the panel shot this question: 'Why do you want to join TISS.'

I blurted out, 'Sir, I am interested in social work. I was a Scout . . . I am totally interested in serving people, . . .' After I offered some more reasons why I wanted to join the institute they thanked me and declared the interview over.

Two days later the list of those who cleared the interview was put up. Neither Guru nor I had got admission. I then happened to meet a new acquaintance I had made at the institute— a chap called Chengappa from Coorg. He was selected.

When I met him the previous day, he had said that when it comes to admissions only influence works. 'I got a special recommendation from the Ramakrishna Mutt in Calcutta where my brother has some contacts. Dr Wadia apparently is very much impressed by the Mutt and the work it is doing. So, I think I will get admission.'

I went back to my sister's house in Bombay totally crestfallen. She tried to console me saying I could try again next year. Meanwhile there were calls from Bangalore urging me to return home immediately My thoughts then went something like this: 'Why should I go back? What awaits me in Bangalore but the courts and all that dreary legal work? I am not interested in going back.'

My sister Lakshmi was terribly worried. Her concern was that a young fellow like me could go haywire hanging around in a city like Bombay. On their part my parents did not want me to be a burden on Lakshmi.

Finally, I made up my mind to go back and reserved my ticket on the train at the end of the week. I was crestfallen but still with a lingering hope that I could make it the following year.

On the day of my departure, the train was to leave around 2 p.m. The previous night I had slept fitfully and tossed and turned in bed. Through the night I questioned the Almighty: 'God, why have you brought me up to this point and then forgotten me?'

But then, out of the blue, another thought came to me. It occurred to me that I had not done one thing which I was duty bound to do. I had met Dr Wadia when I first came to Bombay, I met him again when I was not called for the interview. He had stood by his promise to put me on the interview list. It was another matter that I was not selected because of my poor academic record, or I because I performed badly at the interview. But whatever the reasons, the least I could do was to thank Dr Wadia for the opportunity he had given and say, 'Sir I have failed this year. I will come again next year.'

This thought flashed through my mind repeatedly. So, I went early in the morning to Dr Wadia's house and knocked at the door. He was surprised to see me. I said 'Sir, I have come to thank you.'

He was taken aback. 'But you didn't get admission.'

I said I wanted to thank him despite that: 'You did so much for me. When I did not get the interview call you saw to it that I got the opportunity, but I failed. Obviously, there were better students, so the institute has selected them. True, I did not get selected, but that is no reason why I shouldn't thank you for the kind courtesy you extended.'

He thought for a moment and then called me inside and made me sit down. He asked me several questions about my family background, Finally, he said, 'Okay, do one thing. Go meet Iyer this evening and pay the fees. You are admitted.' I couldn't believe my ears. Before I could even thank him, he added, 'But you will be admitted to a specialization called social research. After having talked to you, I think you will fit in there. Now go and join.'

I went to my sister's home, jumping joyfully. She initially thought I had gone mad because I had not got admission and was behaving strangely. But finally, I convinced her that I had indeed made it to TISS. I rushed back to the institute to pay my fees.

I happened to run into D. H. Guru there. I casually enquired about his plans, 'I have decided to stay on in Bombay. I am not going back to Bangalore,' he said. He had joined Sydenham College for his M.Com. Then he asked me my plans. When I said I had got admission in TISS he was totally taken by surprise.

When I look back, I think the entire sequence of events was just providential. It was nothing but God leading with a divine helping hand that made me listen to my inner voice which urged me to go and thank Dr Wadia. I guess that and my parents' blessings and the values they inculcated in me was what helped me secure my admission in TISS.

A Heart-Warming Response

In 1961, as part of my postgraduate curriculum, I was placed for training at the Leprosy Clinic of KEM Hospital in Bombay. When I reported there on my first day, I sat along with the others waiting on the benches placed outside the doctor's cabin. She was the person who would serve as my guide during my training.

When I met her and introduced myself as the trainee from the Tata Institute of Social Sciences, she asked me 'Where were you waiting till now?' When I pointed to the benches, she instructed me henceforth to sit on the chair in her cabin and not on the benches outside. To my shock she explained that those sitting outside were patients at various stages of leprosy and that some were afflicted with the lepromatous form which was highly infectious.

That came as a bit of a surprise to me because all of them were well dressed without any apparent signs of the disease. The doctor later explained to me the various stages of leprosy and how it can be cured and how some strains are highly infectious when one came in close contact with those afflicted.

What she told me disturbed me since I was commuting by bus and train. I suddenly imagined patients carrying the infectious strain rubbing shoulders with me. However, I overcame this apprehension after learning to take precautions like frequently washing hands with medical lotions and taking a daily bath with an antiseptic added to the water. Thanks to my supervisor after a few days of explaining, I was free from fear.

As part of my training, I was asked to make house visits to a Western Railway porter, a patient under the care of the clinic. The visits were to assess the living conditions of the family and to arrange a medical examination of all the members of the family to detect if any one of them was infected.

After three visits and tests, it was thankfully revealed that only the lone earning member of the family, namely the porter, was afflicted with leprosy, and that it was curable with proper treatment. The visits were also to counsel the patient and other members of the household to take preventive measures like not mixing their clothes with that of the patient's, using separate utensils for cooking the patient's food and other precautions to prevent direct contact.

The family lived in a one room chawl or tenement. The only separate space available for the patient was in the small balcony. During the visits to the patient's house, I learnt that he was not receiving any remuneration since he was on long medical leave. I checked if there was any obligation on the part of the employer to support an employee affected by leprosy. I studied the Leprosy Act and discovered that every employer was legally bound to bar an employee affected by leprosy from attending work. But he had to be kept on the rolls on special half pay till declared cured to join duty.

I asked the patient to accompany me to the Western Railway divisional office to meet the manager on an appointed date. Armed with the Leprosy Act, I explained to the manager the employer's legal obligation to provide half salary to the leprosy affected employee, and that the porter should be put on special sick leave. The manager after perusing the quoted provisions of the law, agreed to issue an order sanctioning special leave with half pay for the entire period when the worker was certified as suffering from leprosy.

When I came out of the manager's office and met the worker-patient and gave him the news along with the copy of his appeal accepted by the officer, tears flowed from his eyes. Though he felt like hugging me, he stood away from me lest he infect me. He then took me to a nearby pan shop, ordered the shopkeeper to open a bottle of Fanta and hand it over to me. He was cautious not to touch the bottle even while expressing his gratitude for my efforts.

I took leave from him asking him to follow up with his office to collect his arrears of pay since I was going to Bangalore for a fortnight. He asked me the details of the train I was taking, the coach number, and the station at which I was boarding the train. I gave him the information although I wondered why he was so curious.

Two days later I reached Dadar station about 15 minutes before the train's arrival. As soon as I alighted from the taxi, four porters surrounded it, trying to pick up my luggage. They ignored my protests assuring me that it is their duty to serve me. I was worried about the charges they may demand hence I was trying to hold them back.

And then one of them said, 'Sir we know you are a good man who takes care of the poor. We cannot possibly commit the sin of charging you for this little work we are privileged to do.' Totally surprised I looked around for some clue when I noticed my patient standing on the steps of the station with an expression of gratitude.

I came to know that he had mentioned in detail how I had taken up his case, making house visits, comforting his family, counselling them, and getting him sick leave with half pay from the Western Railway. His porter colleagues on getting details of my departure to Bangalore wanted to meet me to express their appreciation for the help given to their colleague.

With great affection four of them carried my small bags. As soon as the train arrived, they escorted me to my sleeper berth, spread my bed sheet, placed the pillow, gave me two bottles of water, showed me where my bags were placed and to my embarrassment touched my feet and left. They refused the money I tried to offer them and waved goodbye as the train departed.

My fellow passengers were all astonished at the drama that had unfolded before their eyes. I then had to reveal the story behind what had just transpired. I hoped it made them understand the value of helping the needy and the rich dividend it pays in terms of gratitude, respect, and affection.

Good Intent, Bad Outcome

As a student of Social Research at TISS I was assigned to study an area of Bombay near Bandra called Kherwadi. It was named after B.G. Kher, the second chief minister of the erstwhile Bombay State which then comprised of the present-day Maharashtra and parts of Gujarat.

To enter Kherwadi one had to navigate a wide sewage channel, and cross at a point where a temporary wooden bridge was in place. The objective of my study was to trace the origin of the settlers of the area, their source of livelihood, the community network etc. The exercise was part of my course and the subject of a thesis that I had to submit.

I found that the sewage channel literally surrounded the entire area. On investigation I found out that this was deliberately done by the residents to enclose the area in which several hundreds of hutments, semi-permanent houses and some permanent dwellings were situated. The history of the residents was quite interesting. The settlers were mostly poor migrants from Rajasthan who had come to Bombay. They earned their livelihood by making or repairing footwear, hand bags and the like.

The then Chief Minister, B.G Kher was a very well-intentioned man. He took a sympathetic view of the settlers and decided to improve their lot. He allotted them the vacant land adjacent to the Bandra railway track and provided each family with simple housing, built a mandir and a centre to train the settlers in using modern leather technology. He hoped that with this initiative the poor 'Chamar' migrants would be self-employed and equipped with skills that would improve their economic lot.

During my regular visits to Kherwadi for over a month I learnt two things. Firstly, Mr Kher had perhaps not realized that possession of any land or even a shelter in the centre of Bombay would command a very high price in the future. Secondly, the peripheral swampy and uninhabited area adjoining Bandra provided a perfect cover for brewing illicit alcohol and other illegal activities.

The Rajasthani migrants began to exploit the opportunity. Instead of getting trained in leather technology, they put up hutments around the free housing provided by the government and moved there and rented out the houses allotted to them. Then some others seeing the demand for cheap illicit liquor started brewing it. And to make it difficult for the authorities to check on their activities, they diverted the foul-smelling open sewage to surround their settlement like a moat of sorts.

Consequently, the dream of Mr Kher to improve the lives of the poor migrants from Rajasthan ended up becoming a law-and-order problem for the police and the excise department.

A similar situation was perpetuated in central Bombay where Mr Kher, sympathizing with the plight of Bombay municipal workers, built multi-storied single room tenements with common toilets for them at Jacob Circle. After the tenements were allotted, absenteeism from work among the workers increased. Around the multi-storied buildings, hutments also began mushrooming.

This peculiar trend came to light while conducting a study in 1964 to assess the cost to the government for providing housing to families with an income of less than Rs 500 per month. However, interviewing any householder in the multi-storied flats was impossible as they were always out. It posed a challenge to me to figure out why no householder could be contacted. I had to hang around the area and befriend the tea shop owners and panwalas to understand why.

It was revealed that the situation at Jacob's Circle was the same as it was in Kherwadi. Since housing was at a high premium in central Bombay, almost all the municipal workers who were allotted flats had rented them out and moved to hutments around the multi-storied buildings. The tenant was strictly instructed not to answer any questions from strangers. If anyone were to ask for the owner, they were to merely say that he /she had gone out.

The money the workers earned from renting out their tenements was more than the salaries they earned. This resulted in mass absenteeism, and the area mushroomed with hutments surrounding the multi storied single room apartments.

There was a lesson to be learnt in this. Merely building infrastructure cannot uplift the lives of the poor and marginalised. Bringing about social change is a slow process which requires constant follow up. One good deed does not always result in a good outcome unless it is backed by an effort to change mindsets and give people the inputs required to benefit from that deed.

V

Managing Risks and Challenges

A Bold Move Pays Off

It is truly said that power corrupts and blinds the winner. An electoral victory sometimes brings out the worst in the winner who begins to believe that he or she should be assertive and push ahead with their real agenda that was so far kept hidden from voters. This can happen after any election—be it to choose a trade association chairman or a college union president. It is then up to the more conscientious to object to any move driven by self- interest rather than for the common good.

In 1962 I was in the final year of my postgraduate studies at TISS and was involved in student union activities. One bright student, Ivan Mathais, had approached our group prior to the union elections requesting us to elect him as the president. His plea seemed honest and rather straightforward; he was already a topper in many subjects and if he was elected as the students' union president it would enhance his chances for being considered for the best student of the year award. His frank and no-nonsense pitch impressed many of us and we decided to support him. He was elected.

Soon after the election Ivan's attitude changed radically. He was no longer the simple-minded person he had presented himself to be. He started openly demeaning the previous committee members, which included me, claiming we were all incompetent in running the union. He even began boasting that he would amend the byelaws of the union to make it strong and effective.

In this context he issued a circular prior to the general body meeting of the new union proposing amendments to the constitution, mostly empowering the president to overrule the members. Ivan, it became clear, was not democratic and was keen to exercise his authority.

Perhaps to seal his authority and to silence any opposition he cleverly announced a grand function to inaugurate the newly elected body. Using his connections in the church he invited the Bishop of Bombay, to be a special guest, The director of TISS and all faculty members were invited to grace the occasion. A well decorated stage was setup for the function.

Once the programme began, Ivan made an emotional welcome speech. At one point he referred to an old saying that 'The kite of success flies against the wind of adversity and not with it.' His message was very clear—he would push ahead with his agenda despite any opposition. Following his speech, the director and other guests spoke about TISS, its reputation and how its students can make a difference to society at large. Then the guests were felicitated.

One would have thought that the function had concluded. But Ivan sprung a surprise by calling the meeting to order and announced that the proposed amendments to the constitution of the students' union would be taken up next for consideration and voting. Prior to attending the function, a good number of final year students had agreed to oppose the proposed amendments at the general body meeting (GBM) as and when it was held.

But Ivan had outwitted everyone by converting an inaugural function into a GBM. The students were all dumbfounded in the presence of the distinguished guests, including the director and faculty members. They did not know how to react in front of them and did not wish to be seen as disrupting proceedings. That, many felt, would show them up as undisciplined and could work against them.

Ivan smelt success and moved the first amendment for voting. I was determined to oppose his move to subdue members. I stood up and raised a point of order. Suddenly there was utter silence. Ivan gingerly asked 'What is the point?' I asked him to clarify whether the continuation of the meeting was an extension of the inaugural function or a formal meeting of the general body.

The whole assembly was curiously silent. Then Ivan announced that the GBM had now commenced. I stated that I was objecting to that and explained that a GBM cannot be held in the presence of non-members. I proposed that we formally bid farewell to the honourable guests and reassemble to hold the GBM.

Ivan tried to rule out my objection and the faculty advisor to the union Mr Kaikobad tried to support him by pointing out that even parliamentary proceedings are witnessed by non-members from the gallery. At this stage a large numbers of members stood up to support my suggestion. Sensing that something was amiss, the director and the other guests stood up to leave. Amid the eerie silence, the guests vacated the venue, leaving both Ivan and Mr Kaikobad red faced. The general body meeting also ended without any further transaction.

For the next three days the institute was abuzz with the news that I would be dismissed from the institute for my act of indiscipline. All my friends showered their sympathies on me and promised they would stand by me and even go on strike if needed. But some students felt that students going on strike in TISS would affect its reputation worldwide. I was, to be frank, very disturbed. I knew that if I were to be dismissed, I would be letting my parents down.

Amid all this confusion, I was summoned by the faculty advisor. His call sounded like a doomsday bell to me. When I met him, he was visibly angry and admonished me saying I have 'affected the reputation and dignity of the institute in the presence of guests.' He also pointed out that the director, Dr Gore, felt very embarrassed but he was magnanimous enough to ask me to meet him. I was advised to go and apologize.

I met Dr Gore. He received me with a smile and asked me to sit down. 'Sir, I apologize if I have hurt you, but that was not my intention,' I said at the very outset. To my surprise he responded rather genially, 'Padmanabha you did not hurt me, but hurt my vanity perhaps.' He then patiently heard my explanation on why I had protested. He finally remarked 'What you did was right. It needed courage which you have demonstrated. Please retain that quality in you'. He then inquired about my family and appreciated my upbringing which made me stand up against what was blatantly wrong.

The stand I took against Ivan, which Dr Gore appreciated, worked in my favour seven years later. When Dr Gore met Dr John Wyon, who was looking for a competent researcher for a Harvard University project in India, he recommended my name. Dr Gore even shared with him the strength of character I showed at the union meeting. His recommendation helped me strike a good rapport with Dr Wyon.

First Job Blues

After completing my postgraduate degree in social research, I hung on in Bombay for six months looking for a job. My classmates who had specialised in personnel management were getting employed gradually. Those days Rs 400 per month was considered a good starting salary.

Meanwhile, my mentor Dr Ramachandran advised me to take up a temporary assignment of interviewing foreigners departing from the country at Bombay airport. The job required me to go to the international airport between 20.00 hours to 04.00 hours, and report to the immigration officer. The interviews were needed by the Government of India which was surveying the opinion of foreign visitors leaving the country to assess their views about India— how comfortable was their stay, food and transport? Did they encounter any problems? How was their interaction with people and whether they would recommend India as a destination to their relatives and friends back home? I also had to record any suggestion they had to offer.

I was paid Rs 2 per interview and there was a quota of interviews per night for each country. This was to ensure each day's interviews were spread over many countries. Starting from 8 pm till 4 am, I would average about 30 to 40 interviews a night. The immigration officials were very friendly and cooperative in guiding the exiting foreigners from countries on my list to meet me before they stamped their passports. This helped me to identify my prospective respondents easily and some of them had to wait if I was engaged with another respondent.

I was getting by on this temporary assignment when I received a telegram asking me to report for work. This took me by surprise because I had not applied for the job as a research supervisor in the department of anthropology at the Karnataka University. Apparently, it had contacted the Tata Institute to recommend a suitable candidate to conduct research on welfare activities in Hubli and Dharwar and my name was recommended.

Armed with the telegram, I went to Dharwar where my immediate bosses—Professor Mohanty and Assistant Professor Siddiah— met me and put me up at the university guest house. I was told that four field investigators would be reporting to me.

Three or four days later I was given a formal appointment letter which stated that my position was a temporary one for two years and I would be paid a consolidated salary of Rs 400 per month and that no accommodation would be provided.

On the first day I reported for work, I reached the department of anthropology around 9 a.m. To my utter dismay there was no one around. The chowkidar was amused that I had come to work so early. He said offices opened only between 10.30 a.m. and 11 a.m. So, I went back to the guest house and returned at 10.30 a.m. and waited for an attender who turned up half an hour later. He opened the department and let me in.

A little later my bosses arrived and leisurely introduced me to the four field investigators. Professor Mohanty showed me to a big table in a large hall and asked the four investigators to occupy chairs around it. The professor explained details of the project to be completed and updated us on the work done till then. I was utterly disappointed that no document on the objectives of the study, procedures to be followed, time schedule for the project and budget break up were ready. When I expressed disappointment about the working facilities and modalities, Professor Mohanty apologetically admitted that they had not given much attention to those aspects.

Since he was going on leave from the next day, he asked me to feel free to use his cabin till he returned. It had enough space and facilities to accommodate me and the four field investigators. After his return he promised he would facilitate a more permanent arrangement for us.

So, our team began working on the project. About three days later while we were engrossed in discussing details of the project, someone dressed in a three-piece suit suddenly opened the cabin door and looked strangely at us. The four investigators were shocked. They stood up and whispered to me that the gentleman who had barged in was Professor Eswaran, head of the anthropology department, who had just returned from a foreign tour. I stood up, greeted him, and introduced myself as the newly appointed research supervisor. He obviously took umbrage to the team and I using the cabin because he shouted at the top of his voice that this was not our cabin, Then, he banged the door shut and went away.

Shocked by this rude behaviour, I calmed down my colleagues and asked them the way to Dr Eswaran's office. I was told that it was on the upper floor. I immediately went up to see him. I was asked to wait but I ignored his assistant. Instead, just as Dr Eswaran had barged into our cabin, I pushed my way in and confronted the big man. 'Dr Eswaran I cannot accept the way you talked to me and my colleagues. Since no space was arranged for me and my team to work from, it was on Dr Mohanty's advice that we were using his cabin. I am surprised that the university and your department has appointed me without so much as providing me working space. As for your shouting at us, I find it unacceptable. The least you could have done was to ascertain why we were using the professor's cabin.' Having had my say, I banged the door and left. Ever since, Dr Eswaran was careful while dealing with me.

On the work front I realised that though the research project had been on for six months before I joined, nothing substantial had been done. The work was haphazard without basic research methodology being followed. So, I discarded the work done and decided to start afresh.

But four months into my stint at Dharwar I got a call from my mentor at TISS, Dr Ramachandran. He informed me that the research project I had designed as a student for the National Buildings Organisation had been approved and finances released. He wanted to know if I wanted to direct the project. My salary as the research officer in Bombay would be Rs 350 a month.

I accepted the offer right there and then over the phone. I then submitted my resignation to the Karnataka University. But when I went to return all the project documents handed over to me when I took charge, I found no one wanted to take it back or relieve me. Frustrated I went to the registrar who asked his administration superintendent 'to do the needful.' But he flatly refused to accept my resignation insisting that three months' notice was required.

When I reminded him that the University had appointed me via a telegram without stipulating any conditions, he shot back angrily, 'Employers can impose conditions, but employees cannot make any demands.' I reminded him that I was also a law graduate and that I did not agree with the sweeping statement he had just made. I told him that I would be leaving by the evening train to Bombay and that I would be taking the keys to my desk with me since no was relieving me. I also added that I would be dispatching the documents with me by parcel.

Later I bundled the documents handed over to me and booked it by registered post to the registrar and left. I went to Hubli, a station before Dharwar, to catch the train to Bombay. But when the train stopped at Dharwar, an office clerk from the university came to take my signature on the relieving order and take the keys to my desk. He told me if I was not officially relieved, the University could not appoint my replacement. I had the last laugh.

Seeing Dirt Instead of Seeing God

If you don't look you don't see. Or to put it differently, you see only that which you look for. Indeed, should you look for the negatives in a person, place, or thing you are most likely to find them. It is another matter than in the process you will miss the good that also resides therein.

This great lesson in life was driven home to me by my mother while I was at the Tata Institute of Social Sciences, Bombay. And the beauty of it was that it was communicated by her rather inadvertently and not with the intention of enlightening me. But such lessons, as it always happens, have stayed with me for the rest of my life.

It so happened that I had to go to the holy city of Benares or Kashi to attend a conference of social workers. On learning that I was going to a place considered by Hindus to be the holiest of holy spots, my mother urged me to bring back prasad from the Kashi temple. I assured her that a visit to the Kashi Vishwanath Temple was very much on my itinerary and that I would bring the prasad with me on my next visit to Bangalore.

On reaching Benares, I did visit the famous Kashi Temple, but I was not impressed. In fact, I was disgusted by the crowd of dhoti-clad pandas (priests who double up as guides at religious places) pestering me. Some had lit beedis in one hand and pooja items in the other as they offered their services for a fee that ranged from Rs 5 to Rs 15 for a darshan of Lord Shiva and a variety of poojas.

I settled with a panda to accompany me to the temple. As I moved towards it, I visualized a very high pedestal on which an impressive Shivlinga stood before which the devotee could prostrate and offer prayers. To my utter disappointment, I saw the linga on the floor with many devotees and pandas lunging forward to touch the idol and sprinkle water, leaves and flowers on it. The entire area was very filthy and made me aghast. I thought to myself is this how one worships? I wondered why we humans create such a dirty environment even for God. Finally, I felt relieved when I settled the fee with the panda and took back the prasad packed in an old newspaper.

On my return to Bombay, I put the prasad in my suitcase and forgot all about it. It would be another fifteen days before I could manage a trip to Bangalore. The minute I reached home my mother rushed to me and asked excitedly if I had manged to go to Kashi. When I said I had, she immediately demanded her prasad. 'Okay, okay I will give it you, but I can't understand as to why you ladies make such a big fuss over Kashi.' I then started recounting my experience.

She stopped me in my tracks and asked me a second time, 'Listen, have you brought the prasad? If you have, then please give it to me first.' I opened the suitcase and brought out the prasad wrapped in the newspaper and gave it to her. With great reverence she took one little piece of the sweet and put it into her mouth and fed me the other piece. Then she closed her eyes and folded her hands as if she was in the presence of God.

Finally, she turned to me and said, 'Okay, you can now tell me your *Purana* (epic story).'

I narrated all that I had experienced and how dirty and terrible the whole place was. I said my visit to the temple was disgusting and very disappointing. She stunned me with her response: 'You see son, this is the difference. I was stuck in Bangalore but requested God to send me prasad. He has promptly answered my prayers and sent it to me. But you went all the way to Benares, focused on the dirt and forgot to see God. The result is, you only saw the dirt and came back.'

I have never forgotten what she said and still remember the message that lay hidden in her precious words. I often mull over them and remind myself that in life you can see what you want to see. In fact, my mother's words of wisdom comes back whenever I lose focus or when I am led astray from what should be my goal.

In Bombay's Redlight Zone

In the 1960s a visit to Bombay's redlight area was not for the meek. There were enough scare stories doing the rounds about criminal gangs who ran the show and of murderous pimps to scare most law-abiding citizens. But my work did take me to that 'forbidden' quarter of the city.

It happened when I was the research officer in charge of a survey to be conducted on the rent paid by families with incomes less than Rs.500 per month and their socio-economic profile. The study was sponsored by the National Buildings Organization, New Delhi, and conducted by TISS. Armed with questionnaires my team members were supposed to meet residents and collect data from select places in Bombay identified as clusters of low-income families. One of these clusters was in the redlight area.

One morning Pandit, one of our research investigators rang me up. He said he was afraid of going alone to the redlight area notorious for its nefarious activities. I asked him to wait at a mutually agreed spot and reassured him that there was nothing to fear. I would accompany him.

Once I caught up with Pandit I located a doctor's clinic in the area. I met the lady doctor who practiced there and requested her help after explaining the nature of the work we were doing. Our primary concern, I told her, was that we should not be mistaken for customers.

She immediately sent word for a woman leader of the area, who arrived in fifteen minutes. We were introduced and I explained to her the purpose of our visit. The doctor requested the woman to escort us to the houses already selected randomly from the map of the area. She told her to ensure that when we visited the houses, the inmates treat us with respect and help us in collecting the data which merely related to demographic information and some questions relating to their income expenditure.

The woman leader accompanying us was curious about the survey. She began talking in Marathi to Pandit. She then casually asked me where I was from. When I said from Bangalore, she switched over to Kannada with a distinct Dharwad accent. Her friendly demeanour and interaction were such that it made us comfortable and slowly removed our apprehensions and our preconceived notions about the nature of the people who lived in the redlight area.

As soon as we approached one of the houses on our list, women of various ages colourfully dressed and wearing loud lipstick, rushed out to greet us. Our escort waved her hand and indicated that they go back in. We were then taken and introduced to the madam of the house. The purpose of our visit was explained to her. The introductions over, the first thing the Madam did was to offer us tea which we politely refused.

She then went on to answer all the question Pandit asked. The madam wondered if our survey would lead to houses being allotted to people in the area. We explained that our purpose was to assess the amount of money the government should be prepared to spend if people with poor income were to be provided reasonable housing in Bombay.

The madam and the person escorting us said that though the work we were doing was well-intentioned, they may not see the houses allotted in their lifetime. They then talked about how they, like countless others, had been fed pipe dreams and brought to Bombay only to eke out a living in the redlight area. They said the money they earned was a pittance once rents were paid, commissions shared with agents, bribes paid to the police and protection fee to the gangsters of the area, Then, there was money spent on cosmetics and recurring medical expenses. They hoped that the government would provide reasonable housing which would be of great help.

After visiting the houses earmarked for us, we returned to the clinic and thanked the doctor and our escort for helping us complete our survey within a day. The lady doctor asked me about our experience. I said that while we were apprehensive of being accosted by undesirable elements, the response from the people in the area, particularly the women, was very warm. They treated us with respect, and some even shared their problems with us and how they yearn to live normal lives and be part of the mainstream which shuns them.

Both Pandit and I felt that the experience had opened our eyes to the plight of a section of society that is ignored and lives on the margins. We also reflected upon how we were wrong in our baseless assumptions about the people who live and work in the redlight area.

Personally, it taught me that if we communicate with people with good intent and without fear or bias, they reciprocate with warmth and without fear or bias.

VI
On the Job and on the Move

My Tryst With Destiny

In 1969 I landed a permanent job with the Planning Commission in Delhi as a research officer at a government institute. The job was permanent although it was downright boring. People trooped in late at about 11a.m. and left early by 4.30 p.m. No real work was being done and no one seemed too bothered about that. Much of the day was spent indulging in loose talk or sharing gossip. To me it felt like a dead end.

Just when I thought I had enough, by God's grace, I got an opening out of nowhere. A gentleman—Dr John Wyon, left his card in the mailbox of the barsati (the room on the terrace of a house) where I was staying. He said he wanted to meet me. I didn't know who he was but met him, nevertheless.

Dr Wyon was director of a Harvard University project in India and was conducting research on population. My name had been recommended by Dr Gore, director of the Tata Institute of Social Sciences. When Dr Wyon told him that he was looking for a researcher to join his team, he had recommended me as a suitable candidate.

Dr Wyon offered me a job as a behavioural scientist on his team and I decided to take up the assignment after resigning from my permanent government job. When I mentioned my intention to my father his advice was simple and straightforward. 'I don't know your subject. I don't know what you are doing and what are the prospects. But please remember you are in a permanent job with the government. Before leaving your current job, consult people who know about this subject and then take your decision. I am with you always.'

I decided to resign from my permanent job and joined the Harvard Project at first in Khanna, Punjab. But as luck would have it, we were supposed to conduct a big project in Medak, Andhra Pradesh. So, I was shifted there. I enjoyed my new job, and everything looked hunky dory.

I got married in 1970 and my wife Uma joined me at Medak for a while and then went back to Bangalore. But my comfortable existence was suddenly disrupted in March 1971 when the Indian government ruled that all American institutions in India must discontinue operations by March 31.

Consequently, I was suddenly without a job. My first son Prasanna had just arrived, and I did not know how my wife and I would manage. I was totally devastated. Harvard University gave me some money as compensation for loss of employment and I shifted to Bangalore not knowing what I was going to do.

In September 1971 I got a call from the legendary Dr Kurien offering me a job as scientific officer at the Amul headquarters in Anand. I went there for an interview which went off well. But there was a catch. 'You can join us, but this project is subject to Indian government approval,' I was told. Apparently, the India Development Agency in Switzerland was providing the funds for the research project and under the new rules the government had to give its nod.

Imagine my predicament—I had just lost my job and the new one being offered was shaky. If the government said no to the project, I would be rendered unemployed and would have nothing to show as my professional achievement or experience. Anyway,

I returned from Anand after seeking some time to confirm my acceptance.

I came to Bombay to my sister Lakshmi's house. When I reached there, I was surprised to find an inland letter addressed to me. It was from my friend Chengappa who had written to me from Guntur. He had sent the letter to my sister's address in Bombay, because he did not know where to contact me. He said he had decided to get in touch with me after he read the news that the Harvard Project had been terminated by the government.

Chengappa went on to say that the National Tobacco Company (NTC) he was working for was looking for someone from the Tata Institute who could take up the job of personnel officer at its Guntur office. Seeing this as a godsent opportunity I took the flight to Vijayawada the same day and headed to Guntur.

The next morning one of the directors of the company met me. The only question he had was this: 'Look you don't know anything about industries. You don't know anything about industrial legislations. You don't know Telugu. You don't know tobacco but still you want to venture into taking up the responsibility. How do you explain your decision?' I admitted that all he said was correct, but I believed I had the requisite knowledge which only needed to be applied. 'I have passed my LLB, so I suppose I can understand and interpret law relating to any situation which includes the industry. The other factor in my favour is that as a researcher from TISS I have always been associated with people and interacting with them at various levels. Therefore, industrial relations which means basically dealing with people will not be a problem. As far as tobacco is concerned, I suppose I will get your guidance and I will pick it up in no time. The same goes with Telugu—I will be comfortable with the language soon enough. It shouldn't be a big problem. I think I will manage.'

He then popped the question, 'Do you like Guntur?' I was very frank, 'I hardly know anything about Guntur but whatever I have seen is quite okay. I like the people I have met here They are straightforward.'

I got the job!

I had never thought I would land a job in Guntur of all places. In retrospect, I believe there was the hand of God behind all that transpired. Otherwise, I can't explain how Chengappa wrote that letter when he read the news that the Harvard Project had been wound up by the government. Equally intriguing was the fact that the letter was delivered at my sister's residence on the very day that I reached Bombay after a disappointing job interview in Anand.

A lesson I learnt from the entire experience was that we as mortals may with the best of our knowledge plan our moves in life, yet there is a divine plan protecting us and shaping our destiny.

Some people call it fate. I call it destiny or the hand of God.

Conscience Resides Within Us

Human beings, irrespective of their social status, has ticking within their inner selves a conscience. It urges them, among other things, to come clean and admit their mistakes rather than carry their guilt with them. Of course, there is no scientific proof to establish that the conscience exists. However, there is empirical evidence that surfaces every now and then that confirms its presence.

I learnt this from an incident which happened in the late 1960s. I was at that time a behavioural scientist with the Harvard University Centre for Population Studies and based in Khanna, a town in Ludhiana district of Punjab. I was sharing a rented house along with Dr John Wyon, director of the Centre's operations in India, and the field director, Dr Helen Gideon.

A Punjabi domestic help —whose name I can't recall—used to work for us as a housekeeper of sorts. She used to run the house, cook our food, and wash our clothes. Since we were busy at work all day, we left things under her care, and we trusted her.

Those days I had a set of two beautifully embroidered Swiss handkerchiefs which I treasured a lot. It was gifted to me in the 1950s by Mr and Mrs Bianchi, our Swiss neighbours in Bangalore. I had carefully preserved the kerchiefs all these years and had carried them with me to Khanna. It was in my suitcase and when I took them out one day, I noticed that they looked dull and a bit soiled.

So, I gave them to our domestic help with instructions to wash and iron them and give the kerchiefs back to me. I soon forgot about them as I got busy with my work. A week later I was transferred to Medak in Andhra Pradesh, where the Centre had an establishment.

In the hustle and bustle of shifting, I had no time to remember the kerchiefs. However, three months later I got a letter written in Hindi from the domestic help. Since she was unlettered, someone had written it on her behalf, probably her daughter.

It started out with the usual salutations and then came to the point. 'Sir, I want you to kindly pardon me because I am guilty of a big mistake,' the letter said. 'You gave me two beautiful handkerchiefs to wash and iron. But I didn't give them back to you since I felt they were a good gift to give my daughter at the time of her marriage. So, I quietly kept them back, but my guilt has been worrying me. I have been telling myself that I have done this to someone as nice as you. I want you to please pardon me,'

I was so touched by her honesty that I wrote back to her saying how happy I was to receive her letter and that I was equally happy to know that the kerchiefs served as a gift at her daughter's marriage. I wished her and her daughter Godspeed.

I thought she could well have kept silent on the issue. I had anyway forgotten about the kerchiefs. Perhaps even if I searched for them later, I would have given up thinking I had misplaced them or that they got lost in transit.

But this woman had taken the effort to trace my address in Medak and got a letter written on her behalf seeking forgiveness. This to me was evidence that all humans, irrespective of their social status and wealth, have a conscience residing deep within. In fact, there are those among the well to do who brush aside their feeling of guilt. Not this woman. I felt it was courageous on her part to own up. I shall always remember her for that.

Finding My Feet

After my research assignment with the Harvard Project in India was prematurely concluded, I was forced to go searching for employment. I have already recounted how I landed the job as the personnel officer at the National Tobacco Company (NTC) thanks to my friend Chengappa who also happened to be my boss in the company.

In my new assignment, I had three labour welfare officers reporting to me. My job was complex in many ways, and every day was a challenge professionally and personally. Of all the challenges I was confronted with, I am narrating a few that ultimately tested my management skills.

Perhaps much of the difficulties I faced was a result of my inexperience. I had landed in a job without any exposure to personnel management, industrial law and to tobacco—the product that NTC dealt in. Added to that were factors like my inability to converse freely in Telugu, the local language, and my lack of exposure to trade unions. Moreover, I had just shifted to Guntur with my family which had to adjust to the new place.

On the work front the challenges I faced initially were many. I had to deal with complaints from employees, respond to government notices, address complaints from managers of indiscipline among workers and evaluate requests for assistance from employees.

Unable to understand and figure out ways of dealing with several issues, I used to carry the papers home with the hope that I would be able to deal with them at home more conveniently. But being ignorant and hesitant to act for fear of making mistakes, I used to carry the papers back to the office only to bring them back in the evening with some more pending work. My wife, Uma, with a child to take care of and another one on the way, was obviously stressed for lack of support from me on managing the home.

I soon started suffering from stress related issues like gastric problems, indigestion, and lack of sleep. I even began talking in my sleep, ostensibly discussing various problems at the factory and the office with Uma. She finally confronted me: 'Look I am not aware of the problems you are facing in your job. And yet you keep asking me questions in your sleep. Your health is getting affected but I do not know how to help you. Is there something I can do?'

I was touched by her concern and understood her predicament. I asked her to give me two-days to find answers to my problems. The next evening, after returning from office, I went up to the terrace and meditated. I asked myself the question, 'What is happening to you and where can you find a solution?' After struggling with the question for a while, I concluded that I was fearing the unknown. Further I figured that the solution lay in seeking help from those already in the field and then to start taking my own decisions.

I immediately started contacting mangers and lawyers of other companies to clear my doubts. Very soon I managed to get my confidence back and stopped carrying office work home.

I also had to sort out the problem I faced with the three welfare officers under me who thought of me as too raw and unfit to be their boss. They were all far more experienced than I was. Ramakrishna Rao, a graduate in labour welfare and personnel management from Andhra University with nearly seven years in CTC took care of labour issues in establishments in North Andhra Pradesh, including the tobacco redrying factory at Bikkavolu. Naidu, a retired government labour officer was responsible for handling trade union issues and for liaison with the government in Guntur. And Tilak, a state chess champion selected by the managing director, himself a chess enthusiast, handled labour matters in South Andhra Pradesh.

To make matters worse, soon after my friend and boss Chengappa left CTC, I was put in-charge of the personnel department. Ramakrishna Rao was upset with this management decision and understandably so. As he saw it, I was a person with no formal training in personnel management. So, to show me up he started throwing problems at me without suggesting any solutions.

When I realized that he was cut up I decided to take the problem head on. I went to the Bikkavolu unit to meet Rao. After evading the issue, he finally confirmed that he felt the management has done injustice to him by putting me in charge of the department. I conceded that I understood the hurt he felt and that if I were in his position, I would feel the same.

But I also told him that by blaming the management and letting matters drift he was only proving that the decision to bypass him was right. Instead, if he were to act professionally and keep the company's interest on top and get the productivity moving, he would be proving the management wrong in ignoring him.

I also impressed upon him that I came to NTC to find a job for myself and not to rob him of his opportunities. This open talk mellowed him, however he failed to raise his level of competence.

Tilak was just a happy go lucky person, with a carefree attitude towards his job and responsibilities. Strictures from superiors did not make any difference to him. He loved his *paan* and chewed on it all day. The first time I talked to him face to face and went home, my wife was surprised at the red colour sprayed on my shirt. It was Tilak's contribution to our conversation! From that day, I always insisted he sit on my side and not directly opposite me while conversing for fear of the red spray! Anyway, I manged to work out a friendly working arrangement with him.

Naidu was also a happy go lucky man. Adverse comments on his work were like water off a duck's back. Once when I confronted him with complaints from various quarters of him not responding or reacting to complaints and suggestions, he astonished me by enlightening me with the methodology he followed while dealing with petitions.

His table, he explained, had four drawers. Any complaint or petition sent to him requiring his attention would be placed in the lowest one. If the matter was important enough, he would be reminded by whoever sent him that complaint or petition. Then he would promote the document to the third drawer from the bottom, but he would still not take any action. If the matter was raised again by the affected party, he would move the document to the next drawer.

Only when people complained vociferously and agitated over an issue would he finally act. Incidentally, he told me that any petition lying in the lower drawers for more than three months would be destroyed. This he said, was the way all government officers deal with complaints since many frivolous petitions were sent to them.

After gaining confidence in my handling of the personnel department, the management of NTC in Guntur, including the director D.K. Sinha and leaf manager Peter Laffrey gave me additional charge of the personnel administration of the Leaf Division as well.

About a year after I took charge, D.K. Sinha (DKS) asked me if there was anything that I had observed in the personnel administration of the Leaf Division. I said I had noted that the company had categorized managers in two categories—leaf and non-leaf with the former being given perks denied to the latter, This I felt was discriminatory.

For the benefit of readers, leaf managers were those who dealt with the purchase, storage, and processing of tobacco. All other officers, viz, accounts, administration, personnel, and stores, were placed in the non-leaf category. All leaf managers, irrespective of their rank, were provided perquisites like house, furniture, gas, and reimbursement of electricity bills. Non-leaf managers were not provided any of these benefits. So, I took up the cause of non-leaf managers and said that this discrimination should go.

DKS tried to justify the special perks by noting that leaf managers had to move from place to place. I told him, 'Mr Sinha we abhor the apartheid policy in South Africa, but when we notice a similar discrimination under our very nose, we turn the other way.'

My words had its impact. After three months Peter Laffrey called me and said, 'Paddy I have good news for you. You and accountant Ramaswamy will be given the perquisites on par with leaf managers. I responded by saying, 'Peter, by extending the perquisites only to the two of us, we are hurting the others. I was not suggesting that only two of us should get the perks. In fact, through this decision we will alienate the rest of the non-leaf team. Hence please forgive me, I cannot accept the offer, unless all officers are treated on par.'

As a result, the furniture allotted to me remained in the store. Ramaswamy took his allotment, saying we must take whatever is given by the company and not raise issues. To my delight, six months later all non-leaf managers were extended the perquisites on par with leaf managers. This stand taken by me made the personnel administration team's sense of belonging stronger and cohesive and we developed mutual trust.

Insensitive Circulars From the Top

Those who work in offices must be familiar with circulars issued by the top bosses. Some serve a definite purpose and are often necessary. Others are informative and allows the management to officially communicate a new policy or initiative to its employees. But there are still others through which the bosses vent their anger and frustration. These often have an adverse and demoralising impact on the staff. Many of the circulars in the last category may not have been issued if wiser counsel had prevailed.

Two circulars very early in my career remain fresh in the memory for the wrong reasons. The first of these was in the late 60s when I was working as a research officer with the Central Institute of Public Cooperation in New Delhi.

Those days it was normal for me and two other colleagues to work late in the office when some research assignments were pending completion. On such occasions, all admin staff would leave the office by 5 p.m. while we continued to work in our cabins. The normal practice we followed was to inform the watchman to close the office while leaving.

One day, out of the blue, we received a circular from the director of the institute marked to all staff members. It read as follows: 'It is shocking to note that someone stealthily entered the Director's room yesterday after office hours and ransacked some important and confidential papers kept in the drawer. This is a serious matter. Hence in the interest of office security, the following procedure must be followed henceforth by all those staying back after office hours. Those who wish to stay back to work should compulsorily sign the special register kept with the security at 5 p.m. and also sign the same at the time of leaving with time out recorded. The watchman will be responsible to get the signatures of the staff staying back in the register. This procedure comes into force with immediate effect. All staff members are required to acknowledge the circular with their signature, indicating time and date.'

When this circular was brought for my signature, I wrote on it as follows; 'The reported incident is as distressing to me as it is to the Director. However, I would henceforth refrain from staying back in the office after 5 p.m. lest someone plays a similar mischief and I be questioned because I stayed back.' One of my other colleagues also signed under my note endorsing it.

When our response reached the director, he was furious. He summoned us to his chamber and admonished us. 'You guys should grow up. How can you write a rejoinder on a director's order?' I requested him to examine the situation dispassionately and explained to him that whoever stealthily entered his room would find it convenient to do so again when other staff members are staying back after signing the late register. The person perpetrating the act will be safe while those working late would be under a cloud of suspicion.

As an alternative I suggested installing an alarm on his door and on the table with the drawers which would sound in the event of an intruder entering his office or tampering with his desk. After hearing us, the director withdrew the circular because he probably realized it would dissuade people from staying on in office and doing good honest work.

Another circular which I found rather strange came my way when I was personnel manager at NTC in the early 1970s. The director of the company who had come from Calcutta was alarmed at the quantum of electric bulbs drawn by managerial staff for domestic use. Incidentally, free bulbs were issued as a perk to executives.

Looking at the unusual numbers of bulbs purchased he questioned the store keeper, who reported that the bulbs were issued to officers of the company. Without a second thought, the director shot off a draft circular addressed to all officers which read thus: 'It is noticed that domestic bulb consumption by the officers is abnormally high. All officers are hereby advised to use the bulbs with great care.' The draft was sent to me to be issued immediately.

I took the draft to the director and sought his indulgence to re-examine it. Though annoyed that the new personnel manager was raising objections, he nevertheless agreed to listen to me. I told him that the circular would have a negative impact since the persons misusing the perk would think that all his colleagues were also equally guilty. And those who were honest would end up feeling upset that they have received such a circular.

When the director asked me for a solution, I assured him that we could identify those misusing the perk by studying and analysing the issue register. This would reveal the names of those who had drawn large number of bulbs during the year.

Though he felt it may be laborious—all such exercises were done manually those days—I assured him that we can get a report together in three days. A team of four clerks were assigned the task of identifying the number of bulbs drawn by each officer during the previous twelve months.

The result was astonishing and opened the management's eyes. Three officers related to each other had drawn a total of over 1000 domestic bulbs, whereas the rest of the officers had drawn between five and fourteen each. It transpired that the guilty trio were drawing excessive number of bulbs to distribute them freely among their relatives or for some other reason. The director thanked me for stopping his circular and getting to the bottom of the problem.

Since all the three were senior officers with good knowledge of tobacco, they were let off with a 'Director's advice.' But later, one of them who was the biggest bulb culprit, was dismissed for misappropriation of company funds and other frauds.

VII
From the Guntur Diaries

Remembering Father

In 1976, when I was employed in Guntur, my 77-year-old father had come to Hyderabad to attend a ceremony to mark his father's death anniversary which was being held at an uncle's residence. I met father at that function and requested him to come and spend some time with us in Guntur.

After some persuasion he agreed. Once in Guntur, my wife Uma took meticulous care of him ensuring all his needs were taken care of. Most of the time I was away at work. Despite wanting to be back home early to be with father, given the workload, it was simply not possible.

After a day of his arrival, father resumed his morning walk. He would go out and come back by breakfast time. By then my children Prasanna and Anand would have left for school and would come back only at about 4 p.m. Left to himself father felt a void. He had in recent years started learning Sanskrit but needed someone who could share his interest in that language and its literature

Consequently, after five days of his stay with us, father started enquiring about train timings to Madras. The hint was clear—he wanted to go to Madras where my brother was living. In Madras and Calcutta, two cities he had earlier visited, he managed to cultivate some friends with interest in Sanskrit during his morning walks. He had not struck any such friendships in Guntur and was frustrated.

I felt helpless and tried to find ways to ensure father spent some more time with us in Guntur. The person I tapped for help was Vishwanatham, an assistant in the export division of our company who was very resourceful. I discussed the problem I was faced with and sought his assistance in finding a suitable person interested in Sanskrit who could keep my father company.

Vishwanatham's response came as a welcome surprise: "Sir, my brother-in-law is the principal of the Sanskrit College here. We can meet him at his college and request his help.' I immediately went with him to meet the principal. He shared his name—Anantharamiah—with my father's and was open to meeting him although he had his reservations about how well they would get on. 'I don't know how to interest a person of that age who does not know Telugu. But I do appreciate your good intentions and shall do my best,' he said.

His words were very comforting to my agitated mind, and it was agreed that he would be picked up by my driver around 4.30 p.m. the same day and taken to my house to meet father. As I left the Sanskrit College campus, I was excited and brimming with the energetic feeling one gets when a solution has been found to a problem.

When I informed my father of the plan, he was sceptical of my move, but said, 'Okay, let us see after he comes here.' What transpired after the two Anantharamiahs met was way beyond anything I had imagined. After they talked for half an hour in the drawing room, my father asked Uma to arrange for two chairs and a small table on the terrace and have the lights turned on. He also asked her to send tea and snacks upstairs.

When I returned from office around 7.30 p.m. the two were still engrossed in conversation unmindful of the time. I was delighted at this unexpected response from my father and thought surely God had worked in my favour.

From that day, for about a month, the two Anantharamiahs met every day. They sat on the terrace enjoying each other's company along with the tea and snacks Uma thoughtfully served. In fact, the two became so close that they even decided to see the Telugu film *Tenali Ramakrishna* at the local theatre with the principal translating the dialogues for father's benefit!

When my father, responding to my mother's concerns, decided to go back to Bangalore, principal Anantharamiah sprung a surprise. Knowing my father's interest in Sanskrit humour, he commissioned a group of his students to search and collate humorous anecdotes, quotations, and poems from books in the college library. Then they put together the collection and had it printed in a matter of fifteen days.

My father was invited to the Sanskrit College where he was honoured by the students and teachers who were astonished at my father's enthusiasm for learning at his age. He was then presented the book. My father promised to return to Guntur the following year.

I owe a debt of gratitude to principal Anantharamiah for humouring my father in more ways than one! Of course, this was yet another occasion in my life when I found an unseen hand fulfilling something I needed.

Next year, my father asked my younger brother Vijaya Simha to book his train tickets to Guntur. But a day later he asked him to hold back booking the tickets without giving any reason.

Meanwhile, in February 1977, the staff association of NTC declared a strike protesting for better wages, Supervisors, accounts staff, drivers, and subordinate employees all joined the flash strike. I was the only senior manager holding charge of the unit.

When the strike was declared the previous day, the personnel officer Ramakrishna Rao was admitted to hospital with a heart ailment. And the government labour officer had issued notice for a conciliation meeting for the next day.

On the day of the conciliation meeting, I got a call from my sister Vani at 4.30 a.m. that my father was admitted to hospital after a suspected heart attack. I asked her who among our nine brothers were there attending to father. She said five of them were present at the hospital. I explained the situation at the office and told her that I would be in touch with her every hour to know father's condition and would try reach Bangalore asap.

Since I had to attend the meeting with the labour officer at 9 a.m., I asked my wife Uma to call up Bangalore every hour and keep me posted. Since there were no mobile phones then, I asked her to call the factory manager Shivaji who would in turn pass on her message to me at the meeting.

When Uma kept ringing every hour updating me about father's condition, Shivaji learnt that despite a personal crisis I was attending the meeting called by the labour officer. Meanwhile, unexpectedly, the company's director Mr Sinha had arrived at the factory. He was unaware that the staff was on strike. He also learnt that my father was admitted in a Bangalore hospital and that his condition was serious.

At the conciliatory meeting called by the labour officer I had taken a tough stand and refused to yield to the unreasonable demands of the staff. The meeting broke up and I returned to my office where the factory manager informed me that my father's condition was stable, and that Mr Sinha was in Guntur and was in his office.

Still reeling under mental pressure because of the strike and my father's condition, I rushed to meet Mr Sinha. I was taken aback by the first question he fired at me. 'Paddy, what are you doing here?'

he wondered. Visibly upset to hear that from him, I retorted, 'What do you mean Mr Sinha?'

'I understand your father is in a serious condition in Bangalore, so I was wondering why you are still here,' he said.

I was humbled by his concern. I quickly updated him on the crisis in the company and how there was no one to take charge if I left for Bangalore. He said that I needn't worry on that count. 'Now that I am here, I will take care of things. You must get going to Bangalore at once or you will regret it all your life.'

Mr Sinha then asked the factory manager to arrange for a taxi to take me to Bangalore. He did not even want me to waste time giving him details about the strike. I rushed home by which time the children had been brought back from school and Uma had served lunch for us.

Just as I was going to the washroom, I broke down and cried uncontrollably. Uma came to console me. Meanwhile the phone rang, and I was told dad had breathed his last just then.

Whenever I recall that day, the entire sequence of events still surprises me. Surely, the omnipresent God had come to my assistance in my hour of crisis. That alone could explain Mr Sinha's unscheduled visit to Guntur and his taking charge of the factory. What's more, why I cried uncontrollably just when my father passed away has remained an enigma even today.

Money vs Integrity

When ownership changes it shakes up most organisations. No matter how smooth the transition, the new management brings with it its own style of functioning. This was what happened at the National Tobacco Company where I served for ten years between 1971 and 1981. When I joined the company, it was owned by B.N. Elias & Co, a Jewish establishment. Later in 1980 it was acquired by the Goenka Group. After the change, policies and priorities changed. The new management it seemed, were more focussed on pushing the company's earnings.

Anyway, when the takeover happened, I was the commercial manager responsible for all commercial operations including the export of tobacco. Among other things, the change in style of the new management also called for compromising personal integrity and showing your loyalty to the company.

On both counts I drew my strength from my father. His definition of integrity and personal values were soon put to test in my job. It had to do with the scrap generated from tobacco leaf which was sold to beedi makers of Gujarat. It was an important source of revenue for the company. Under the previous management I, as the commercial manager, authorized the sale of the scrap and made entries in the book.

But after the Goenkas took over, the director I reported to called me and said that hereafter tobacco scrap sale must be a cash transaction which must not be entered in the company books. 'We will tell you whom to give it to or how to spend it,' I was instructed.

I looked at the director and said, 'Sorry this is something I cannot do. I don't work for any individual. I work for the company, and I would not do anything without entering it in the company's account books.'

The director didn't get upset or angry. He simply said that was okay. But then he added, 'I can understand that you don't want to do it, but do you mind if some other manager handles the money from the sale of scrap in cash?' I said I had no objections. 'I have no problem. I am not here to teach anybody morals. So long as the money transaction does not require my signature, it is okay by me.'

At that juncture I was to go to Japan. It was my first trip out of India, and my presence was required to inspect the tobacco supplied to the Japanese company, which was our client. Just before the trip, I was called to Hyderabad by the company's director, Mr Jain. He said "I am happy that you have manged to instil confidence in the Japanese, so we thought you should go for the inspection trip to Japan. Meanwhile, I want to tell you that we have decided to make you director of three of our group companies.'

I was quite taken aback since it was a promotion from commercial manager to director of three companies in the group. It was by any reckoning a major jump. I thanked Mr Jain for reposing so much faith and confidence in me. I was rather pleased with myself.

But Mr Jain was not quite done with me. 'Before you go you must sign some papers so that we can open accounts in the banks. My secretary Paul will tell you what needs to be done. So, complete the formalities today before returning to Guntur.'

Paul, Mr Jain's secretary, came to me with the bank forms. 'Please sign here —but one thing—don't put your normal signature. Sign in different names in each of these bank documents,' he instructed. I was intrigued by why that had to be done. Pat came his explanation: 'We are opening the accounts in different names, and I will take you and identify you as say Janardhan, Dodde Gowda or some such name in each bank and you sign as that person before each bank manager. Hereafter, when you conduct transactions with each of the banks you have to remember in which name you have opened the account there.'

I left the papers with Paul and went to meet the director. I said, 'Mr Jain, I am sorry. If this is what you want me to do, I am not the person. I cannot do these things and I won't do it. Even if you ask me to quit, I will be happy to leave the company rather than open illegal bank accounts.'

He was immediately apologetic. 'No, no, why do you think I will ask you to leave? It is okay. If you don't want to open those accounts, we will ask somebody else to do that.'

As the Japanese visit was due, I told Mr Jain that he should ask someone else to go on that trip since I would be looking for a job in Bangalore and would be moving out of Guntur. I also pointed out that he must have lost his confidence in me since I had refused to open fake bank accounts.

He implored me not to cancel my Japan visit. 'No, no, no, why are you linking the bank matter with your trip? The Japanese have confidence in you, and you should go and see that the inspection is done,' he said.

I assured him that I would go ahead with my Japan trip. But as soon I came back, I fixed a job in AEG NGEF (New Government Electrical Factory) in Bangalore. So, I quit National Tobacco. There was a one-month gap before my wife and kids could shift to Bangalore and the director of NTC took personal care to look after their wellbeing in Guntur.

A little after I left the company, the directors and managers of National Tobacco were rounded up by a government enforcement agency and put in jail. Those who I had advised not to take illegal steps like forging signatures or receive company monies without issuing receipts were all arrested. Mr Jain and Mr Goenka were taken into custody in Calcutta.

Some of my colleagues regretted that they had not followed my advice. 'Sir, we should have listened to you,' one of them said, 'We ended up in jail. We are still being called to the courts and our life is ruined.'

I thanked God and my parents who had embedded in the minds of their children the value of integrity in life. That, I believe, was one of the reasons why I was not lured by the promise of making easy money.

Jacob the Humble and Lovable

My days in Guntur bring back a flood of memories. Some very poignant and touching. One narrative that remains fresh in my memory involves Jacob, a member of my personal staff.

Well, it so transpired that when my boss Chengappa at NTC left the company in 1971 to join the India Tobacco Company (ITC), I took over from him as the head of the personnel department. While he was with NTC, Chengappa had a handyman in his personal employ who helped his wife Mangala in the kitchen, did odd jobs in the house and ran errands for her. His name was Jacob and Chengappa had taught him driving and even got him a licence.

Since Jacob was rendered jobless after his employer left Guntur to take up the new assignment, I decided he was a good man to have around the house. Jacob could be a great help to my wife Uma and the children. As things stood, the added responsibility of heading a department weighed heavily on my inexperienced shoulders and I had little time to spare for home management.

So, I employed Jacob as a company driver for my car and he also doubled up as a handyman for Uma and the children. Looking back, I reckon it was God's plan to usher in Jacob into our family. He instantly endeared himself to my wife and kids. That came as a great relief since I had to travel on work, and I could do so knowing that the trustworthy Jacob was there to take care of every little thing in the house.

The kids loved him. In fact, it was amusing and heart-warming to find Anand—he was about three then— calling out to Jacob when I or Uma shouted at him. On such occasions, he would run to get cuddled by Jacob and seek protection from him.

Jacob got married in 1972-73 and a son was born in 1974. He came to give me the good news and sought my permission for what he obviously thought was a delicate matter. 'Sir, I want to seek your permission.to keep my son's name as Anand. Will you permit me to do that?'

I was amazed by his request. 'Why do you need my permission?'

'Sir, it is like this,' he explained, 'You trusted me enough to look after your son Anand. And now I wish to name my son Anand so that "Anand" is always with us.' Jacob was a devout Christian, yet what he considered important was the pure emotional value of our relationship when he chose a Hindu name for his son.

Even after we left Guntur Jacob regularly kept in touch with us over the phone and never missed greeting us on New Year. Though he came from a very humble background, Jacob had uncorrupted honesty, sense of responsibility and humility in his personality. I witnessed these qualities being publicly recognized when he retired as a driver from the Andhra Pradesh Commercial Taxes Department.

Jacob had rung me up and requested me to attend a function arranged by his department to bid him farewell. I could not resist the emotional temptation to be present on the occasion. The function was an eye opener to me. The department had put up a pandal, and the jeep he had driven till his retirement was positioned next to the dais. The vehicle was clean and shining as if it had just come from the showroom.

Jacob's colleagues in the department and their families were all there at the function. What was astonishing was that several of his bosses whom he had served years ago were present. They were now in high positions at various places in Andhra Pradesh but had come to Guntur to wish him well. It was evident that the humble Jacob had been a role model for his superiors also!

After the farewell function, Jacob pulled my heartstrings yet again when he requested me to accept his invitation for dinner at his modest house. When I reached there, I found he had invited some of our contacts in Guntur from yesteryears, his relatives, and pastors from his church. After I was introduced, all of them prayed for the welfare of my family and a long life. Knowing that I was a vegetarian, Jacob had ensured that a special meal had been prepared for me.

I was deeply touched and moved. I understood why it was said that values that are cultivated through one's cultural upbringing and selectively acquired are more precious than any commercial richness. Jacob's life was a testimony to that.

Sugunamma's Genuine Concern

Many of us come across various situations in life when we suddenly realize that persons who we hitherto took no notice of are indeed noble and compassionate souls. Through their one act they suddenly rise in our esteem, and one can't help but admire them for their selfless empathy and kindness. Such people may be simple folk who don't have the trappings of education, power or wealth but may be deserving of much more respect than their station in life affords them.

The story I am narrating happened on the day workers struck work at the factory of the National Tobacco Company in Guntur where I was in charge. Between 1000 to 1500 agitating employees had gathered at the main gate at about seven in the morning and I got a call from the labour welfare officer alerting me on what had happened.

He sounded rather disturbed and advised me not to use the main gate to enter the factory. 'There are thousands of workers who have collected there, and they are very agitated. They are demanding higher wages,' he said.

I told him that there was no need to panic. 'I will go in from the front gate,' I said.

'No sir, you please come in from the back entrance,' he insisted. 'We will keep it open. There are no protestors there.'

I told him that I had no intention of making a back door entry. So, I reached the front gate in my car. There were employees in their hundreds shouting anti-management slogans. As the car reached the gate the crowd surrounded the car, and my driver was a little unnerved. I told him to stay calm, roll up the windows and not to react.

The sloganeering continued for about ten minutes. Meanwhile, one of the workers who was drunk, took a big stick and hit my car's dickey. I think that it was at that point that the leader of the protestors realized that things were going out of hand. He knew me as a person who would not harm workers' interests. In fact, in the past we had discussed several issues faced by the employees and even worked on possible solutions. He now came and stood in front of the car and asked the others to give way. 'We have made him aware of our demands so let him go inside. He will then call us for a meeting and if the issues are not settled by the evening, we can consider further action,' he told the workers.

The car was let in, and I reached my office safely. Meanwhile, my distressed wife Uma had rung up the labour welfare officer enquiring if all was well. He had informed her that after facing some protests at the gate, I had reached my office safely.

Later I got a call from Uma to tell me that Sugunamma, our domestic help, had rushed to our house and told her that she had learnt that 'Sahib had been beaten up near the factory.' Uma reassured her that all was well—that there was some *galata* (trouble) but I was safely inside my office. 'Don't worry, somebody seems to have given you wrong information,' Uma had told her.

But Sugunamma was not convinced and urged my wife to call me again. Finally, I had to confirm to Sugunamma that no harm had come to me. I also told her that things like strikes happen, and she should not get so agitated.

When I went home that afternoon Sugunamma was waiting for me. She came up to me said, 'Sir, I heard about the problem. I was so disturbed I was praying to Jesus all the time to keep you safe. Now I want you to do me a favour. In the evening could you please come with *ammagaru* (madame) to my small house. I have called our padre from Vijayawada (about 40 km from Guntur) to pray for you.'

I was so touched that I agreed to be there with Uma.

In the evening Uma and I reached her hutment dwelling. She had invited many Christian workers from the factory They were all huddled together holding lighted candles and praying for our family's safety and welfare. We were so moved by Sugunamma's gesture that we could not hold back our tears.

It was very difficult for us to understand her concern. We were hardly paying her much for her work and yet she was paying us back many times over with her genuine love and concern. Her innocent heart was truly connected with ours, and I am grateful to God for having introduced her to us.

Even today I remember her. Her parents had indeed chosen an appropriate name for her. Sugunamma means good natured, and she had proved that goodness had been bestowed in her in good measure.

VIII
The Stint in Bangalore

The Toilet Blues

After I quit NTC I moved to Bangalore as the deputy general manager (personnel and administration) at the New Government Electrical Factory (NGEF). The public sector firm was incorporated in collaboration with the German firm AEG and was hence also referred to as AEG-NGEF.

On the day I joined, the managing director, Mr Menzline, a German gentleman, called me to his office. 'Padmanabh,' he said, 'there is much discontent among the workers. I don't know why they seem so irritated. I want you to please look into it and come back to me after a week and tell me what I need to do to minimize the discontent.'

I started by studying the factory premises and the office building. The MD, general manager and the deputy general managers' offices were on the first floor of the new building, where the toilets were excellent and up to German standards. Then I went down to the staff toilets. They were of the same design but somehow it was not as clean as the toilets on the top floor.

Next, I went around and found a structure called "toilet" for the workmen. I tried to go inside. I couldn't because the stench was so repulsive. Cigarette butts, sand, and broken urinal pieces and broken doors of the toilet stalls were all over the place, and people were still sitting around and smoking.

When I finally persuaded myself to go in, those inside got up, startled at my unexpected presence. I couldn't bear the stink for long. Nevertheless, I went round and came back with my observations. On the seventh day when I met the MD, he asked me what I had found out.

'I want you to come for a tour with me please, I won't tell you anything but please come with me,' I said. He obliged and accompanied me. I took him to the officers' toilet which he also used. He wondered why I was taking him there.

'Please, please, bear with me. Have a look at it.' Then we went to the staff toilets. He wondered what I was trying to convey to him. I pleaded, 'I want you to please hold on and observe.'

He did just that. 'Okay this one for the staff could be a lot cleaner, like the one that we all use, but what is it you are trying to tell me?'

I then I took him to the workers' toilet. He saw but dared not enter. It was as if he was pushed back by the stench that was emanating from inside. He then blurted out, 'Padmanabh, I never knew this.'

I promptly said, 'When people are made to use such a dirty facility their minds also work in a dirty manner. They are irritated because they have no choice but to suffer this place.'

He got my point. 'What do you want to do?' he asked. I pointed out that proper toilet facilities must be built for all the workers. He immediately gave a blanket on the spot sanction to build a new toilet with adequate facilities for workers like the one provided for officers and the staff, with porcelain wash basins, toilets with doors, and urinals.

While we were building the new facility, there were rumours among the workers that the management was again building a separate toilet for the factory managers. I let the rumour flow and after the toilet was ready for use, I got it locked.

Then I called the union leaders for an inspection. 'I want you to please come with me to see the new toilet that has been built,' I told them with pride.

Their response was predictable. 'You mean the new one built for the factory managers?' one of them said.

I quietly took them around and showed the new facility to them. They said it was excellent but wondered who it was for.

'This one is for you guys,' I said and added, 'You take the key now. Providing facilities is the management's responsibility. Utilizing it and looking after it is the users' responsibility, which is you guys. I want you to please look after the facility.' They thanked me effusively.

Just two days after the new toilet was opened for workers, a security guard came running to my office. He said 'Sir, Kottarrappa sat on the wash basin, and it fell down and is broken.' Ten minutes later the union leaders rushed into my office. They said 'Sir, you must sack that contractor. The wash basin fell on its own because it was fitted very poorly.'

I said that they should stop telling lies for something as simple as the wash basin falling. 'I know Kottarrappa sat on it and it broke.' They were surprised that I had the information and so they changed the tune and implored me to replace the porcelain basin with a stainless steel one.

I refused to oblige them. 'I will have a new porcelain one installed but only after you collect four annas from every worker because someone from among you has misused it.' They said that would be difficult. But I insisted that they either pool in the money or I would have to ask Kottarrappa to pay at least 50 per cent of the cost. They went out, deliberated, and came back to say that each worker would contribute four annas each. They thus remitted 60 per cent of the cost of replacing the damaged wash basin.

Then the next day I found the big drum with sand provided for dropping cigarette/ beedi butts was turned upside down so that people could sit on it. But overturning the drum led to sand being strewn all around the toilet. So, I called the union leaders who started apologizing and assured me that such things won't happen again.

I gave them a piece of my mind. 'The truth is this. You may get all the facilities but unless you use them properly, any facility will become dirty and rundown. So, hereafter we will not hear any more complaints about the toilets.' They agreed to ensure there was no misuse.

Predictably, the new toilets did have a positive effect. The production manager from the factory told me that the workers were calmer and more relaxed. Thus my 'toilet remedy' worked wonders for the workers and my German MD was rather pleased.

All about a Car

When I joined AEG-NGEF in 1981, one of the conditions that I insisted on was being provided a company car and a driver. I was told that this was against the company policy, but since I refused to back out the management reluctantly agreed. My argument was that my earlier job did allow me that perk and I would want that to continue.

So, my appointment letter included the clause of providing me a car with a driver. After I joined work as deputy general manager (DGM) (administration and personnel) I noticed that at lunchtime the other five DGMs of different departments would meet in a room adjacent to mine. But I was never invited.

It was not that I kept a distance from them. In fact, I had gone to their workstations and introduced myself to each of them. Following that, we would exchange a hello when we passed each other but none of them even tried to strike a conversation with me. This went on for about ten days.

Though they were cold and polite towards me, I couldn't help but notice that when the five met at lunchtime they would be laughing and cracking jokes like good friends. They obviously did not want to include me in their circle because of some misgivings they had about me.

On giving it some thought, I realized it was all about the car I had been allotted. None of them had been provided a company vehicle and the managing director had told me as much when I was interviewed for the job. I reckoned it irked them to see me coming to work in the car and being driven back home in the evening.

However, I was not sure if it was only about the car. So, rather than allow misgivings to fester, I decided to confront them to ascertain the real problem. One afternoon I simply barged into the room where they met at lunchtime. They were totally taken by surprise and hurriedly made place for me to sit down.

I came to the point. 'Gentleman, I have noticed you have some wrong notions about me. I do not know what it is, but there is something you feel that makes you keep a distance from me. Now I see that day in and day out. Why don't you even invite me to join your group at lunchtime or talk to me socially?'

They denied all that vehemently and pointed out that I was surely mistaken. But they did not sound very convincing. It was almost as if they were holding back something and were reluctant to share it with me.

So, I decided to hit the nail on the head. 'I know what the problem is. You see me using the company car and driver and all of you presume that I am misusing my position as DGM (administration) to usurp the official car for my personal use. That is far from the truth, and I would like to clear the air now. Gentleman, let me make the disclosure that at the time of my appointment it was spelt out in my contract that I would be allotted a car and driver. So, I was merely given what I was promised. I have not misused my position to grab a car as you perhaps think.'

However, I did not stop there and quickly added. 'I realize that none of you as DGMs are allotted cars. In fact, I notice you come in your own vehicles. As I see it, you have not been allotted a car because you never asked for it. Since I insisted, it was put in my contract. I admit it is a bit embarrassing for me that only the DGM administration has the facility of using a company-allotted car. In fact, as the person in charge of personnel, which includes managers, I would like to see how this can be corrected.'

They wondered how that could be done.

So, I suggested a course of action: 'We have an executive committee meeting every month, which is attended by the MD, GM, company secretary and all DGMs. I will bring up the issue there and we can try to find a solution. But until then please don't mistake me to be a person who is misusing his position.'

They apologised profusely and said it was good of me to clear the air. Soon after the interaction with the DGMs, I briefed the MD about the issue. I told him that the company had eight cars in its fleet, including the one allotted to me. The seven vehicles were allotted every morning by the personnel officer who had the headache of allotting the cars on a first-come-first-served basis to whoever rang up first to book a car for the first half or second half of the day. Those requesting late when the vehicles were already busy were asked to hire a taxi and submit the bill.

That was the system being followed and it led to conflicts with a department denied a vehicle accusing the personnel officer of favouritism. When I explained the situation to the MD, he agreed to my suggestion to allot a car each to the five other DGMs and one each to the GM and the company secretary. Each DGM could then permit the use of his personal car by others in his department as and when required.

At the Executive Committee (EC) meeting, I promptly brought up this issue stating that car allocation was causing conflict, and embarrassment. I pointed out that the daily allotment of cars had become a headache for the personnel department and proposed that we could sort out the problem if we allotted the five cars to the five DGMs who are not provided company cars. Each DGM would in turn allot his car daily to facilitate the movement of personnel in his department.

The EC approved it saying it was an excellent idea. So, the same day we allotted a car to each DGM. The personnel officer thanked me profusely for relieving him of the daily headache of allotting cars.

Two days later the DGM (marketing) barged into my room: 'You are a clever guy. You transferred the headache of allocating the vehicle for my departmental duties from the personnel office to me. Now first thing I do in the morning is to prioritize movement of personnel and allot my vehicle. It is driving me nuts.'

My response to him was simple. 'Bring up the matter at the next EC meeting with your suggestion to resolve the problem,' I told him.

Needless to say, he never raised the problem.

The Healing Touch

My job at AEG-NGEF threw up one problem or the other which required deft handling. One day the factory manager came rushing to me urging my intervention. 'I have a very serious problem on the shop floor. One of the workers, Lingappa, is a real rowdy and I am unable to control him. Even the workers fear him. He works as a painter and if the supervisor asks him to do his work properly, he pulls out a knife. He even threatens other workers. Please, do something to control him. It is becoming terribly difficult for us to handle him.'

So, I sent word for Lingappa. He came to my office, and I politely asked him to take a seat. But he refused to sit down. 'Tell me what you want?' he said, aggression writ in his voice and added in good measure 'I won't sit down.'

'Unless you sit down, I won't talk to you,' I said firmly.

But he stood his ground. 'I will not sit down. I don't have time. I won't sit down,' he said emphatically. I could see he was very angry and agitated. So, I explained, 'Lingappa, when a worker comes to my office he has to sit down before we talk.'

He continued to be adamant, 'No, I don't have the time to sit down. If you don't want to talk, I am going,' and he walked out. I could gather that he was a difficult nut to crack.

Two days later just as I reached home at about 6 p.m., I got a call from the factory. A driver who had just returned after his day's run was on the line. He said, 'Sir I am driver Peter, there is a lady here who says she is Lingappa's wife, she is crying and seeking help.' I asked him what kind of help? He said somebody had beaten up Lingappa and thrown him in a gutter near Indira Nagar and his wife was helpless.

I asked the driver if he had some money with him. He said he had Rs 100 on him which was quite a bit of money in the 1980s. So, I gave him instructions: 'Peter, you have the company car, right? Take this lady to the spot, pick Lingappa up and take him to the Indira Nagar Hospital. Pay the money you have on you and admit him. I will reimburse it.' He said he would do just that.

At about 9 p.m. I went to the hospital. Lingappa had been attended to. His whole face, except for his eyes was bandaged. So were his arms and legs. I held the palm of his hand and gently enquired, 'What happened, Lingappa?' He did not reply but I could see tears in his eyes. I then spoke to the doctor on duty who assured me that the patient was okay and would be discharged in a few days. After a while I left assuring Lingappa's wife of all help.

Next morning, I told Matthew, one of my assistants, to look up Lingappa in the hospital with a bouquet of flowers. For the next few days, I sent Matthew to call on Lingappa till he was discharged. Later, when Matthew claimed the bill for all the expenses incurred on Lingappa, the accountant raised objections saying that this was against company rules and would set a precedent.

I had a word with the MD who initially backed the objections raised by the accountant. In fact, he pointed out that if the company spent money on Lingappa it would have to cover the expenses on any other employee who gets into a private brawl and gets injured. I explained to him that this case was an exception rather than the rule and that it was not every day that someone gets beaten up. In any case, if cases like this come up frequently then there was something wrong with the company or its employees.

Moreover, I impressed upon the MD that paying Lingappa's hospital bills would have a very positive impact on the workers. They would begin to see the management as one which cares for their wellbeing. The MD, a German gentleman, was convinced by my line of reasoning and the bills were cleared.

About a week later Lingappa reported for work. As per company rules when an injured or sick person resumes work, he must bring a fitness certificate from the hospital/doctor. Lingappa came with the fitness certificate to the gate and said he wanted to see me. I told security that I was busy, and that he should report to the factory manager. But Lingappa insisted that he wanted to meet me first, so I agreed to see him.

He came to my room and prostrated himself at my feet and started crying. He apologised profusely for his conduct. 'Sir, I am sorry that I was neglecting my work at the company. I was creating problems for everyone, but I never knew that the company would take care of me so well. You are like God to me. I assure you sir that from today onwards you will not hear any complaints about my work or my behaviour.' I said it was alright and that he should report for work.

A few days later, the factory manager reported a complete behavioural change in Lingappa. He was not only working hard, but also making people work, helping other workers, solving problems on the shop floor with total dedication.

What I learnt from this experience is that as human resource managers we should seize every opportunity to send a message down the line that the company cares. And managers must act on the spot in the event of an emergency which concerns a worker. You can't waste time over rules and regulations. In this case Peter the driver was not duty bound to report Lingappa's problem to me. However, he responded humanely and admitted his colleague to hospital with his own money.

What was also interesting was the way the mind of an accountant works. In a case like this, if the management were to make an exception to the rule, they fear it will set a precedent. I had to convince the MD that there is something known as discretionary action. In an emergency, managers have to put their foot down and act. That action neither sets a precedent nor does it re-write the rules of the company.

I have been asked if the MD finally backed me because he was a German—a foreigner. But if you analyse what transpired one will see that he first agreed with the Indian accountant, but later was convinced by an Indian HR person. It is not because he was a German that he saw reason but because he had hired an effective HR manager on whose professional reasoning, he was confident to take the call.

A Parking Problem

Egos hurt easily and sometimes over trivial matters that don't warrant an emotional or intemperate reaction. When I was DGM administration and personnel with AEG-NGEF I got a call one day from one of my colleagues, Mr Oglae, who was DGM production.

'Padmanabh, I never thought this company has different rules for different people,' he said rather cryptically and cut the line. I rang him back wondering why he seemed so upset. 'I don't want to talk. You go and find out,' he said without giving me a clue.

'Mr Oglae, whatever it is that's bothering you, let us talk,' I said. But he banged the phone down saying he was busy.

I went down to meet him at the factory and spotted him involved in a discussion with some workers. I went up to him and said, 'Mr. Oglae, I want to talk to you now.' He cut me off saying that he was busy. But I persisted. 'You may be busy, but this is an emergency, I just have to have a word with you.'

Seeing that I was insistent, he reluctantly agreed. To make things easier for him and not to keep him far away from his work I suggested we have a chat in his office. But no sooner had I sat down that he asked me pointedly what was it that I wished to talk to him about. 'Mr Oglae, I want you to order some tea,' I said to calm him down. 'Please order it. Let's have tea first before we talk.'

He said he was very busy. I told him we were both busy, but could he order some tea. Very unenthusiastically he ordered two cups.

Sipping my tea, I asked him what was it that was troubling him. He wouldn't tell me. He said I would have to find out what the problem was. I was intrigued and tried to get an answer out of him. 'Mr Oglae, you have not told me the problem. You simply said over the phone that there are two different rules for different people, right? If you tell me the two different rules, I can find out and correct it.'

Then after few more sips of tea he finally revealed what was bothering him. 'Listen, yesterday my car was parked in the shade next to the admin building and your security officer ordered my driver to take the car away and park it elsewhere. Now go and look at where your car is parked.'

I was surprised, to say the least. 'Mr Oglae, why are you so upset about a simple thing like that? Do you know that I don't know anything about my car being parked there?' To this he simply repeated what he had said all along that I should find out.

I said, 'We will surely find out, but you seem to be accusing me of having instructed my driver to park the vehicle there. Please wait a minute, you just hang on for a bit.'

With that I picked up the phone on his table and called the security officer, Ayyanna. I said, 'Mr Ayyanna, is my car standing next to the admin building in a no parking area?' When he confirmed that it was, I snapped at him, 'Why have you allowed that?' He said that my driver had said he would park there. I was angry. 'I want the car moved immediately and once that is done will you please get back to me.' He called back within minutes to report that the car had been moved out.

I then turned to Mr Oglae and asked him how he had found out about my car being parked in a no parking area. He said his driver had complained to him saying. 'Yesterday the security chaps asked me to move your car. Today AP's car is parked right there.'

'Mr Oglae,' I said, 'You must understand that we are both holding responsible positions and if some people come and give you some information you should not act on it. You must investigate. In this case, the only thing that was required was for you to tell me over the phone and I would have clarified that I had no idea that my car was wrongly parked. I would then have taken corrective action.'

He understood. 'I am sorry, I got really upset this morning when my driver came and said that my car was moved out while your car was allowed parking at the very same spot.'

I gave him a piece of advice: 'You must be aware that people may say things knowingly or unknowingly which create wedges between people at the workplace. We should be conscious of that, and at our level we should be very cautious before we act.' He said he agreed with me and apologized. We became close friends ever since.

Though Mr Oglae is not with us anymore, I often recall this incident because it drove home the point that responsible managers must process information before acting on it. If they don't, one could end up being guilty of jumping to conclusions, creating ill will, or making a mountain out of a molehill.

Trouble in the Canteen

I was in my office attending to work when I heard loud banging from the adjacent building as if a group of people were pounding on a door. The building housed the canteen of AEG-NGEF where at 12 noon shop floor workers came for lunch which was provided free of cost to all employees by the company. The canteen was managed by a contractor.

Since the banging continued, I went down to make enquiries. I was told that it indeed came from the canteen. Apparently, the workers who had gone there found the door locked from the inside and hence they were banging on the door. There was obviously a slight delay on the part of the contractor to get the food ready, which had angered the workers. Luckily the door opened soon, and the banging stopped.

A few days later a security guard rushed into my room. 'Sir, the workers have emptied sambar over the contractor's head,' he said sounding alarmed. I ran to the canteen. Fortunately, the sambar was not very hot, and hence the contractor was safe. When I saw what had happened, I raised my voice at the workers. 'You can't do this. If the food is not good, you say so, and we will look into it, but this is no way to treat people.' My intervention stopped the ruckus, but the workers took the opportunity to register their complaint about the poor quality of food served.

I learnt that the workers, numbering about 150 which included workshop workers, drivers and housekeeping staff went in the first batch at 12 noon for their lunch. Other staff members would go in the second batch at 12.30 p.m. The third batch which included employees in administration, stores and accounts as well as managers were given the 1 p.m. slot. So, I reasoned with the workers that everyone was being served the same lunch. 'You see even the managers have been eating the same food.'

'No sir, it is not the same food. You get different food. That contractor is clever. He makes sure that he serves you good food, but what he gives us is terrible,' the workers alleged.

Listening to them I reckoned it was just frustration at the workplace that was manifesting itself in the canteen. Much like how frustrated husbands find fault with what is served by their wives at the dining table.

Anyway, I started wondering what the solution for the canteen problem could be. I discussed it with Mr Menzline, the managing director and proposed that we could tweak the way lunch was being served so that it becomes apparent that there was no distinction between managers and workers.

I explained my plan. 'We could make each department manager, staff and workers under him go in one batch. This will help all employees appreciate that food supplied by the canteen is the same for all workers, staff as well as managers. Lunch will be served in three batches covering all the workers, the staff, and the managers.'

Mr Menzline held a meeting of all department heads and announced the plan for revised canteen services seeking their consent. He said he would join the third batch for his lunch. The department heads agreed that the intended change would improve the atmosphere in the canteen.

But when the revised plan was announced some of the managers and white-collar staff were upset. They said that that they could not sit with the workers and eat. When I asked them to be more specific one of them said, 'We may not feel comfortable at the way they eat, the way they talk etc.'

I persuaded them to try out the new system for a few days. On the first day there was total silence in the canteen because I and Mr Menzline went and sat with the first batch. I particularly made it a point to sit between two workers. They smiled but were very nervous and quietly ate their food.

The managers and others cribbed for a while but soon stopped complaining. The new system was accepted. So, the problem of indiscipline in the canteen was sorted out. But the quality of the food remained an issue and the union representatives frequently complained about it to the personnel officer.

The issue was further escalated by the worker's union whose representatives met me seeking a resolution. At the meeting my question to them was to the explain specifically what they meant by quality? I explained the problem to them, 'Someone might say the food is too spicy, while someone else may say it is insipid. It is very difficult to please everyone but let us try and find a solution.'

They asserted that a solution was impossible since the 'contractor does not cook properly.' It was a vague charge so I suggested that a worker could be deputed to monitor the cooking. 'You give me one workman from among the 150 we have here. He will be made totally free from regular work and posted in the canteen to select the menu for the day, check the quality of ingredients used by the contractor to ensure quality of the food prepared and to supervise the canteen. Only after his approval will the food be served by the contractor. The workman you select must be in the canteen every day. On days he is absent, the union should nominate a substitute worker, who will be deputed by the management to supervise the canteen.'

The union representatives agreed to this and felt it was a good idea. But when I communicated my plan to the factory manager, he took serious objection. 'What have you done?', he asked me and added, 'You know I will lose 2400 manhours a year by posting a man on canteen duty. How am I going to account for it?' I said I would show him the number of manhours he was losing because of the canteen problem.

I collated the data of production loss due to this problem for the previous two years. It was running to about 7000 to 8000 manhours hours per year. I showed him the figures. He finally agreed and so did the managing director.

So, we gave the responsibility of supervising the canteen to one of the workers. After three days the person assigned to canteen duty came to me. 'Sir, I don't want to do this job,' he said. When I asked him why, he explained, 'Sir, everyone is shouting at me. They are questioning me about the quality of the food and putting the blame on me.' He was obviously under pressure from the workers. But I told him that he must continue his work in the canteen and if he has a problem with some of the workers, he should take it up with the union.

I then called the union representative and pulled him up. 'This is not done. The person you have chosen has been given the job of supervising the canteen and he cannot be taken to task by the workers. You must accept responsibility and keep those creating trouble in check.'

The union accepted my point, and the problem was sorted out. The canteen contractor came and thanked me There were no more complaints about the food.

A Humane Gesture that Helped

I recall it was a Sunday evening in Bangalore and I was driving my car with Uma seated beside me. It was around 5 p.m. when we passed through the main road adjacent to Wilson Gardens on our way to Jayanagar.

The road had sewage lines on both sides covered with granite slabs. While driving past I noticed a man coming from the opposite direction on a scooter riding over the slabs. Suddenly I saw its rider falling into the drain where a slab was missing. I stopped my car and rushed to help the man screaming for help from inside the drain. Several others passing by also rushed to the scene.

We pulled out the victim of the accident who was bleeding profusely, while his scooter was stuck in the gap created by the missing slab. I realized that the injuries sustained were serious and he needed hospitalization. Since I was unaware of a hospital nearby, I sought the help of onlookers. One uniformed policeman in the crowd informed me that the nearest one was the St. John's Hospital in Audugodi. I volunteered to drive the injured man there but sought the help of someone in the crowd to help me carry him to my car.

As soon as I made the request, people lifted the person and made him sit in the back seat. I then requested one person from the crowd to sit with the injured man till we reached him to hospital.

The crowd suddenly disappeared. I asked the policeman present to help, but he left the spot saying that he was now off duty.

Left with no choice, I asked Uma to keep talking to the man so that we could be sure he was conscious and alive. The injured man identified himself as Abdul Sattar from Audgodi and said he was returning home from his cloth shop near the city market when the accident happened.

Soon we reached the Emergency section of St John's Hospital and the attendants there brought a stretcher and took the man inside. A head nurse came and asked us about the incident and how we were related to the patient. On realizing that we were only acting as Good Samaritans, we were asked to write down details of the incident, our names, address, and telephone number.

By that time a nurse brought a small pocket diary recovered from the victim containing names and telephone numbers. The head nurse called up a few numbers and got in touch with the injured man's wife and asked her to rush to the hospital. Since the patient's house was close by, six of his relatives reached the hospital in quick time.

Seeing the blood stains in our car, one of them suspected that I had caused the accident. The head nurse sternly ticked him off and told him of the service rendered by us. After the relatives arrived, the hospital authorities thanked me and Uma and asked us to carry on.

While returning home I noticed the man's scooter still lying where the accident had taken place. To be on the safe side, I went to Siddapura police station and met the sub inspector and narrated the whole sequence of events. I enquired whether I was legally obliged to file a report with the police to avoid any false claims. The sub inspector thanked me for acting like a responsible citizen and took down my phone number and address. He assured me that I would not be troubled in any way. He also said he would arrange for the safe custody of the scooter at the police station.

We reached home late in the night and washed all the blood stains on the back seat. A fortnight later, Abdul Sattar and his wife visited us bearing gifts of fruits and flowers to express their gratitude. We hugged each other and I could see their eyes brimming with tears.

A month later, there was a flash strike in the evening at the NGEF unit in Bommasandra a few miles away from Audgodi. As the deputy general manager in charge of administration and personnel I rushed there to find out what was the problem. I was immediately surrounded by angry workers who had held up busses taking employees back to Bangalore after their shift at the unit was over.

Latiff, a union leader, was standing on a makeshift dais and was condemning the management in a loud and harsh voice. The situation was a bit tense as the employees on the day shift were being prevented from returning home by a section of workers. As this tamasha was going on, I noticed a person with a muffler covering his face passing by on a cycle. He stopped and called out to Latiff who got down from the dais and met the stranger and came back and suddenly announced that the agitation could be called off for now. 'Since our concerns have been brought to the notice of the DGM who is present here, we will wait for a week. If our problems are not resolved by then we shall show the management what we can do.' With that the strike was miraculously called off.

Two days after the incident, I got a call from the security at the main office that Latiff wanted to meet me urgently. I was not inclined to see him but when he requested a few minutes with me I relented. Latiff came to my chamber and instantly fell at my feet. I was astonished at this behaviour from a vociferous union leader. Then he apologized for what had happened at Bommasandra plant two days ago.

When I asked him the reason why he had suddenly called off the strike that day, he said that the person on the cycle who spoke to him during the workers agitation was his uncle Abdul Sattar, the very man whom Uma and I had taken to the St. John's Hospital a month ago. Latiff had obviously been advised by his uncle not to trouble someone who had been so kind and helpful. It was hard for me to believe the strange coincidence which helped me in resolving the agitation. One simple act of helping a fellow human being in need, had truly helped me.

Sattar kept in touch with us till we moved to Bhadrachalam from Bangalore.

IX
The Bhadrachalam Days

The Hanuman Challenge

In 1987 I was well ensconced in my job with AEG-NGEF in Bangalore. My work had become familiar and the challenges routine. To be honest, I had no reason to complain but for the fact that I was a trifle bored with the job. Somewhere in the back of my mind I was hoping for a change, although I did not actively seek it.

It was at that point that I received a call from the Indian Tobacco Company (ITC). The gentleman on the line was someone familiar with my work in Guntur with NTC and had a good opinion about my professional capabilities in handling industrial conflicts and labour issues.

He briefed me about the severe labour problems at ITC's Paper Board unit in Bhadrachalam, Andhra Pradesh (now Telangana). A union leader had been murdered by Naxalites inside the residential campus in broad daylight in the presence of many employees and their families. This had created a created a crisis of sorts among ITC employees and called for deft and sensitive handling.

Having given me a rundown of the situation, the gentleman, an advisor to ITC, popped the question, 'Padmanabha, can you join us as general manager (personnel and administration) at Bhadrachalam?' He concluded the conversation by saying that if I found the offer agreeable, I could meet with ITC's top officials in Hyderabad and mutually discuss the terms.

I was suddenly faced with a dilemma. I knew I was comfortable with my safe and secure job in Bangalore. But on the other hand, ITC was a major corporate entity which was offering me a job. To add to the confusion, my old friend Chengappa, who was with ITC, rang me up and advised me not to take up the assignment. 'It is very tough out there in Bhadrachalam since it is a Naxal area. That apart, the managing director is also a very difficult man to deal with,' he explained.

But I cut Chengappa short. 'Look you and I both handle the personnel department. I feel I should take up the job as a challenge. I like challenges.' He said it was of course my choice and that he was just 'concerned' about my welfare. I told him that there was no cause for worry and that I would first assess the situation and then take a decision.

After I met the ITC management in Hyderabad, I was quite determined to take the new assignment. To resolve conflicts and to bring order in the unit of a company like ITC was an opportunity and challenge for any HR professional. I thought it was worth taking the risk and so I took up the offer.

Just ten days after my joining in Bhadrachalam I faced my first problem when the security officer came running to me and said, 'Sir the workers have smuggled a big idol of Hanuman into the residential campus. They want to install it tomorrow under a tree in the premises. They sneaked in the idol in a car without the security guard's knowledge and it is now in somebody's house.'

I realized that if installing the idol was allowed it would set a precedent. Tomorrow someone will bring in a statue of some other deity and within no time the whole complex would be filled with images of gods. So, I told the security officer that no installation could be permitted.

Then I decided to see where the idol was kept. It was stored in a gunny bag in a workman's house in the employees' colony.

I got the bag opened and told the employees categorically that no installation would be permitted inside the company premises. Mr Chaudhary, the vice president, and my immediate boss who had accompanied me endorsed my stand. 'We can't allow it because any decision to install an idol must be a decision taken by the company management. We cannot allow anybody to do such a thing within the company premises.'

The employees' representative and 40 to 50 of the workers with him seemed adamant. 'Sir, you do what you want. We shall install it. After all, we have gone through a very difficult period, and we want a Hanuman here to protect us and we are going to install the idol tomorrow morning,' he said defiantly.

I urged him to think it over for 15-20 minutes and then we could meet to find a solution. He said the workers had nothing to think over since they had already decided. The representative then articulated the employees' position: 'There can be no other solution, sir. We have already decided. The Hanuman is here, we have paid for it, and we are going to install it.' With that he went away.

I discussed the problem once again with Mr Chaudhary and we both agreed that under no circumstances could we allow the installation. Permitting employees to use the company premises as they wished, we felt, was out of the question.

So, I sent word for the employees' representative and the others with him to meet me. As I waited for them, I was praying to God for a solution. Suddenly I got the strange feeling that I should tell the employees that I would not allow the installation at any cost. That I would personally come in the morning to ensure that the idol was not installed.

And I told them just that. 'Listen,' I said, 'if you are so determined to install the idol, the same Hanuman will give me the strength to come and lift the idol up and take it out of the compound. I will do it physically. You do what you want.'

They said I shouldn't do that, but I was insistent. 'You may hurt me, you may kill me, it doesn't matter. I am going to take the idol out. The same Hanuman will be with me. You will see that happening.' They found me totally determined and so they went out and spent another hour in discussion. They then said they wished to meet me.

Meanwhile, the security guards told me what had transpired during the discussion that the employees just had. The gist of it ran like this: 'This man is a new man whom we don't know. From the way he is asserting himself it seems he will come and disturb the installation. Now we are installing the idol for our good and for our protection. If after the installation this man comes and displaces the idol, it will affect all of us. In fact, it will be bad for us. We may beat him up, we may do whatever, but he seems very determined.'

So, they got back to me and said 'Sir, we have brought the idol inside and we want to install it. But what you are saying is we need the company's permission to do that. We understand your position. But what is the solution? We have told people we are installing the idol. There must be a solution to this.'

I responded by pointing out that they had created the problem and it is up to them to find a solution.

Believe me, a little later the representative returned and offered a solution; 'Sir, you speak to the executive officer of the Lord Rama temple here. It has places where idols are kept in safe custody. So, you could request him to keep the Hanuman idol till such time that the company installs the idol here.'

The Rama temple he was referring to was nearby and the temple authorities held the executives of ITC in high regard. I immediately rung up the temple's chief executive and sought his help. He was most helpful: 'No problem at all, sir,' he said. 'You please send the idol here. We will hold on to it till you seek it back. This is not a big issue—we keep several idols of this kind.'

I made the call at 9 p.m., five hours after I was alerted about the problem. I called the workers and told them of the decision to keep the idol in the custody of the temple. They said they found the solution agreeable but had one request—that they be given a jeep to take the idol from the colony to the temple in a procession. I readily granted their request, and the problem was solved.

They of course got back to me enquiring about when the company would build a temple in the residential campus and install the idol. But ITC has a way of procrastinating when it comes to such matters, and nothing happened till I left the company five years later.

When I came back to Bangalore, I felt uneasy that I had not fulfilled the promise to install the Hanuman idol. So, after about two years, I wrote a letter to ITC reminding it of our promise to the employees. Nobody cared to even respond to my note.

So, I spoke on the phone to one of the employees who had initiated the process of installing the idol and was now in a local bhajan group. I confessed to him my concern and asked him if something could be done to install the idol somewhere 'If you want, I can send you some money,' I said. To my surprise, he said that only the previous day a family from his bhajan group had come to him and asked him if they could take the Hanuman idol and install it and he had given his consent.

I was quite happy that idol would at last find a home. A small temple for Hanuman was built very close to the Rama temple and the idol was installed. I donated Rs 5000 for the installation expenses. After that whenever I happened to be in Bhadrachalam I made it a point to visit the Hanuman temple to pay my respects.

What the experience taught me was that if you are intent on seeking God's help, you will get it. All you have to do is sincerely seek it. I believe God was with me during the Hanuman crisis and helped me resolve it.

The Fruits of Risk Taking

When I look back at my days at ITC in Bhadrachalam, I marvel at how I enjoyed taking risks. I guess it was all about accepting a challenge, resolving it, and emerging with a smile. Indeed, managing risks has always given me pleasure so long as it did not hurt someone bodily or emotionally.

I have already mentioned how I was cautioned by my friend, Chengappa about moving to Bhadrachalam. He had apprised me about the risks involved in working in a Naxal area and that too under a MD who, given his ego, was a difficult man to deal with.

But, despite his warnings, I had gone to meet the ITC management in Hyderabad and had accepted the job as general manager (personnel and administration). At the interview the MD had explained the complex HR situation that prevailed in Bhadrachalam. Then, he asked me if I knew how paper was made considering I was joining a unit manufacturing paper. I confessed that I did not know enough.

'I am surprised that you don't know. Yet you are coming for a job interview in the paper manufacturing industry,' he wondered. I was quick and frank with my response. 'Yes, that does sound rather strange, but I know I am talking to an expert in the field. If I were to claim that I know, you will find me totally lacking in knowledge about paper making, except some rudimentary stuff like it's made from bamboo.'

He was impressed by my frankness and said, 'I like you. You are prepared to say that you don't know boldly and truthfully. I will tell you how.' He then explained how paper was made and at the end of the interview told me that I was appointed.

There were indeed many HR challenges in my new job—an accidental death on the shop floor, unruly workers, Naxal groups putting pressure on the management and a host of community conflicts, some petty and some serious.

Luckily for me, I started my first day by seeking divine blessings without my having planned to visit any place of worship. It so happened that on the day I reported for work, my immediate boss, Mr Chaudhary, the vice president, had gone out and would only be back in about an hour. I was thinking of going back to the guest house and returning later when the personnel manager, Mr Reddy, who was to be my assistant, suggested that we could utilize the time by going for darshan to the Rama Temple that Bhadrachalam was famous for.

I was surprised by the suggestion made by someone who was a veritable stranger. Anyway, I agreed, and Mr Reddy took me to the temple, and we had a quick and wonderful darshan of Lord Sri Seetha Ramachandraswamy. In that temple employees from ITC, particularly the senior staff, were treated with great respect.

After we finished the puja and came out, I remembered I had to buy toothpaste. So, I went to a shop nearby to buy it when I noticed Mr Reddy in conversation with a group of seven men standing nearby. When I came back after my purchase, he introduced each of the seven men by name. I wondered who they were and whether they worked for ITC.

One of the men answered me. 'No sir, we are murderers. The company has accused us of having murdered the union leader.' I was naturally startled by his reply and mumbled, 'Oh I see, anyway good meeting you guys. I hope everything will get settled in time.'

Later I realized that meeting the men was a divine pointer to me that to settle the complex human resource problems at the ITC campus, I needed to tackle the problem related to the seven men I met as a priority. It was a situation that needed sensitive handling.

Three months after I joined, my boss Mr. Choudhary resigned as he wanted to go back to Ahmedabad. Soon after, Mr Chugh, the MD came down to Bhadrachalam from Hyderabad. He summoned me to his chamber and asked me about the HR situation and my plans to resolve them. Then suddenly, he changed the topic and said I must be knowing that Choudhary had resigned. When I replied in the affirmative, he asked me a question which came like a bolt out of the blue: 'Will you take over from him as vice president operations?'

I was shocked and surprised. It was only three months since I had joined ITC and I knew nothing about the paper industry, but here was the MD asking me to takeover operations. I just stared at Mr Chugh in silence for a moment and said a simple 'yes' to indicate that I was ready to take up the challenge.

He didn't appear surprised that I had agreed, but asked me, 'Where do you get this confidence from?'

I said, 'From you, because you have evaluated the situation and feel confident that I can manage this place. The risk is much higher for you than for me. Mine is a personal risk. Yours is a risk for the company. When you are prepared to take the risk to make me the offer, I think I should stand up for the confidence you reposed in me and shoulder the responsibility and handle it. But I need to ask you a few questions. There are three general managers who are technically sound and who are working here for years. Why are you not offering the post to them?'

He said he would answer my question later, but he wanted me to first elaborate on where I derive my confidence. So, I obliged him and said, 'Look it is simple, as far as management is concerned as you gravitate upwards, you are not managing anything except people. You are dealing with people who are competent in their fields and all you need to do is to ensure they are supported to be efficient and productive. So, you are basically servicing and managing people. As far as my experience goes, I have always dealt with people

'Also, take the example of family-run companies where a grandson just 22 years old becomes the chairman. The youngster who has no industrial or management exposure, is appointed chairman, isn't it? How does he manage? Technically he is not trained or qualified to fully understand the nuances of products or services of the business. Yet, he quickly learns to manage people. It is always the other people who produce, and they should be enabled to be efficient.'

Mr Chugh was impressed. 'I fully appreciate your logic. Please take over. I am going to make the announcement.'

I asked him about the other general managers and wondered whether they would be upset by my being appointed over them? But Mr Chugh put me at ease: 'I have talked to all of them, and they are also of the opinion that Padmanabh is better suited to manage the conflicts and problems that we have here.'

Soon after the MD left, I went to meet Mr Venkatraman who was the general manager (technical) for the last seven years. I told him of the offer made by the MD and added, 'Let me tell you, I have not come here to rob you of your opportunities. I came here to do a job, but this happened most unexpectedly this morning. I wanted to talk to you because I will need your help. Without your support it will be very difficult for me to manage.'

Venkat did the unexpected. He got up from his chair, came over, and hugged me. He said, 'Padmanabh, Chug talked to me, and I gave him my yes. I pointed out that for managing people and complex administrative issues at the mill, Padmanabh has better

HR knowledge, experience, and capacity than I have. I told him that I thought he made the right choice and that I will stand by Padmanabh.'

Venkat was always with me. Soon after taking over, I formed a committee with the three general managers, to review and take collective decisions on a day-to-day basis. I was supported by the team, and we had respect for each other under my leadership.

I thoroughly enjoyed taking the risk of handling so important a job. If you look at my performance graph at Bhadrachalam for five years you will see that among other things, I started a community water project which earned ITC a lot of goodwill in the area. My tenure with ITC was a wonderful life experience of immense value.

My take from Bhadrachalam was that one should not shy away from opportunities because of inherent risks but evaluate the risk factor and think of possible ways of overcoming and handling them. Remember, if you don't, someone else will.

The Divine Pull

It was indeed fortuitous that I managed a stint at Bhadrachalam. This became apparent to me when I happened to visit my cousin A.V. Ramachandra in Mysore. At his home I found a little green book titled *Babboor Kamme Yasho Dhimdhima* (The Drumbeats of Babboor Kamme's Success). My curiosity was immediately aroused because it described the origins of the Babboor Kamme clan or sub-sect of Brahmins to which I belonged. It was also my family's social identity.

Babbuekamme were the original settlers in a place called 'Barbara Desha' which later became Babbooru in what was 'Khammanadu' in Andhra Pradesh which is now Khammam district. My ancestors were priests in a big temple of Lord Rama there. When I read about it, I was very thrilled and excited. To me the narrative and my going to Bhadrachalam sounded rather romantic like the *Return of the Native*.

I thought I had been to so many places in India, but it was as if God had just drawn me to the abode of my ancestors—Bhadrachalam. This was amazing. I suddenly realized that 'we can't foresee every detail in God's plan.' But in my case, He had been kind enough to pull me to the very place inhabited by my ancestors. Indeed, to Lord Rama's lap of protection. I knew instinctively that the temple at Bhadrachalam was the one where my ancestors were once priests.

I thought it was wonderful going back to my roots in Bhadrachalam. My only regret was that my parents had by then left for their heavenly abode, and hence I could not provide them the pleasure of Lord Seetha Ramachandraswamy's darshan on earth.

I believe that the book I found at my cousin's house was a divine plan to remind me of my origins. It also served to remind me that I was under the protective hands of Lord Seetha Ramachandraswamy, whom my ancestors had served with devotion. After reading the book, all the warnings from well-wishers about my joining ITC at Bhadrachalam simply evaporated.

Incidentally, the book I have referred to was published by the Babboor Kamme Sangha of Mysore. I still have a copy.

God's Helping Hand

Once I took up the job with ITC in Bhadrachalam, Uma and I were faced with the challenge of ensuring a good education for our children. Since I had to shift lock, stock and barrel from Bangalore to my new place of work, we had to make suitable arrangements for our sons Prasanna and Anand's schooling.

Bhadrachalam was then a small town with limited choice of schools. Anand on an earlier visit to Madras was quite impressed by the Kendriya Vidyalaya inside the Madras IIT campus. So that was an option for him. As for Prasanna, it was decided that he could stay on in Bangalore and be a support to my sister-in-law Rama and her two kids. She had lost her husband, my brother Vijaya Simha, in a road accident and was living alone with her children.

Meanwhile, Anand got admission in the Kendriya Vidyalaya, Madras, with hostel accommodation. Under the circumstances, the arrangement we worked out was thought to be feasible and practical. But the family being separated injected a sense of uneasiness among all of us and we hoped that we would learn to cope with it.

But we did not. Uma had to make frequent trips to Bangalore to comfort Prasanna who was feeling neglected, and Anand stepped up his visits to Bhadrachalam from Madras to be with me. After I noticed the increasing frequency of his visits, I confronted him seeking to know the reason why he was so keen to be with me. On two occasions Anand's response was, 'I wanted to see you. Don't you like it?'

On the third visit within a month, I questioned him saying that he was not telling the truth. On intense questioning he revealed that he was under pressure from his seniors who were drug addicts. The suggestion was that perhaps they were pushing him to take drugs. And then I noticed marks around his waist, which looked as though they were left by someone brandishing a belt like a whip.

But my son insisted that it was caused by falling off a cycle. (Even today I do not know the real cause.) Anyway, without a second thought I asked him to quit the school in Madras. I told him I would seek a readmission to the Bangalore school which he had left recently.

His response, at the age of 16, was touching. He felt it would put a big burden on Uma and me to relocate him to Bangalore. He also said confidently that he would go to Bangalore on his own and get readmitted to his old school. Without another thought I informed Uma and arranged for Anand's relocation to Bangalore. As always, God extended a helping hand in the form of my brother-in-law Anil and his wife who offered to accommodate and look after Anand in their house.

In retrospect God saved us from what could have been a disaster had Anand continued in Madras.

Kumari Reformed

My relocation to a small town like Bhandrachalam had its own challenges on the domestic front too. My wife, Uma, could not always be with me since she had to attend to our children who were pursuing their studies in Bangalore. So, she chose Kumari, a young woman, as a domestic help to take care of my food and housekeeping.

She was a very intelligent woman with two children, a son and daughter to look after. Initially, for a few days she came for work on time and was never late. Uma had instructed Kumari about all the work to be done and my wife was very happy with the dedication our help showed towards work.

However, when Uma returned to Bangalore to be with the children, Kumari became erratic. She knew that I left for office at 8 a.m. and so she made it a point to come after I was gone and let herself in using the spare key given to her. As a result, I used to have some bread or fruits, make myself a coffee and rush to office.

When I came back at lunch time Kumari would have left leaving rice, rasam, a few rotis and a vegetable dish on the table. So, I was left with no choice but to eat a cold meal. The story was the same in the evening. By the time I would return, Kumari would have come and gone leaving dinner on the dining table. She made this a routine, and I did not complain because I never got to see her.

In time I also noticed that small change—4 anna and 8 anna coins—which I left on the table was disappearing. If there were three or four coins, two of them would be missing. I observed this for some time and wanted to confront Kumari.

One Sunday I stayed back home till she came for work. I then asked her to come to the drawing room since I wanted to talk to her about something. I asked her to sit down but she was reluctant. 'I won't talk to you till you sit down. You sit down,' I said sternly. She sat down.

I then posed her a question, 'Kumari, why are you working for me?' She said '*Dabbu kosum* (for money).' I could see she was taken aback by my query.

Then I posed my next question: 'Why do you think I am employing you?' She said she didn't know so I explained, 'You are employed here because I need help. I need somebody to take care of my food, cleaning the house etc. But one thing we should have between us is respect—I must respect you and you should respect me. But unfortunately, I find that I am unable to respect you. The reason for this is because you are not here when I require you. You don't come on time. You keep food on the table and just go away. I have no option but to eat cold meals every day.

'Secondly, I find some coins are missing from the table. Since no one has access to the house except you, I am losing respect for you. Now I don't know whether you have respect for me or not, but I don't see it because if you respected me, you would not be working like this without a care. Have you understood?'

She said she understood what I meant. Then I added, 'If you don't respect me you don't have to work here. Please think of what

I have just said and decide. If I can't trust you, I don't want you here. But if you wish to continue working with me you must make sure that I respect you.'

When I concluded my sermon, I found tears in her eyes. She said she would like to continue working at my house. From the next day the change in Kumari was visible. Not only did her work improve but she also came to me to discuss some of the problems she was facing because of her work timings. 'When I come here my son's school gets over for the day. So, he has to be alone at home without a proper place to study,' she once told me.

I offered her the use of the small room next to our kitchen for her son to study. That small gesture went a long way in changing her attitude towards me and her work. She began taking extra care to ensure that the food was tasty and that the house was kept neat and tidy.

One day in the afternoon I came home for lunch. The driver dropped me and went off to eat his food. After my meal I went to rest for a while in the bedroom upstairs but suddenly developed acute pain in my leg. It was so excruciating, that I shouted for help.

Kumari rushed to my room and wondered what had happened to me. 'I have got severe pain in my leg. Please bring some hot water and give me a hot compress.' She ran down and boiled the water. Meanwhile, she rang up the office and alerted security to send my driver Lalliah to me urgently.

She came back to my room with hot water and a towel and gave me a hot compress. While she was doing it, I noticed tears rolling down her cheeks. I was touched by her concern and have not forgotten the way she helped me when I was seized by the pain.

That day I realized one thing. Kumari was a simple soul with a heart of gold. It took just some talking to and a kind gesture on my part to bring about a change in her attitude. We often prejudge the poor and think that they can't change or that they lack self-respect. This is not at all true.

Till this day Kumari calls us occasionally to enquire how we are. Whenever we visit Bhadrachalam, she comes to see us. There have been five endearing persons like her from Guntur, Bhadrachalam, Bangalore, and Hyderabad who keep in touch. We cannot repay our debt to these people for the invaluable service they rendered, and for the concern they showed towards our welfare.

Conflict Management

When I took charge of the ITC unit at Bhadrachalam in 1991 we had people from the local community gather at the gates requesting one thing or the other. Their demands ranged from water and roads to electricity and employment. The people believed that the company was obliged to address their concerns since they had given their land to ITC. It was another matter that they were compensated for it.

At times frivolous complaints were filed with the local authorities which resulted in notices being served on the company. This I was told was a routine problem and much energy and time was wasted responding to such notices. Being new to a company operating in a rural area, I did not know how to go about handling it. So, for a start I decided to attend the local panchayat meeting to understand first-hand what the community expected from the company.

The vice-president of Bhadrachalam Paper Board was considered almost like a king by the villagers. When I entered, everyone stood up. They were taken aback by the sudden appearance of a top company executive at the meeting. It was the first time such a thing had happened, and they scrambled to find a proper chair to offer.

After I sat down, the panchayat chairman asked me, 'Sir, what made you come here?' I said I had come because I needed help. They sat down and I did some explaining. 'Listen, every day you come and shout at the company gate. We are unable to run the factory. My time is being lost only to attend to this problem of protests and demands. Can you help me?'

They were puzzled by my request and wanted to know what I meant when I said they should help, when ITC should be helping. I elaborated further, 'You demand water, roads, power, etc from us. We pay taxes to the panchayat hence it is you who must provide basic amenities to the company. You should be providing drinking water. You should ensure there is uninterrupted power and that the roads are well maintained. But instead, you come and demand all this from us. Is it fair?' They responded by pointing out that the panchayat did not have money and that it was only ITC which was flush with funds.

Given their position, I quickly thought up a solution. 'Alright, can we do one thing? Please select one problem which we should all get together and solve this year—I mean in the next twelve months. You discuss amongst yourselves and identify the problem. Then we can work on it together with a deadline. I will give you one month's time to get back to me. Tell me when you have decided.'

Having said my piece, I got up and left the meeting. My suggestion made a big difference. The women panchayat members and their male counterparts fought for several weeks over what should be the first issue that must be addressed. Ultimately the women prevailed and solving the drinking water problem was accorded top priority.

The women members had a strong case. They argued that every day they had to access water from the lone company tap meant for the public. Finally, everyone agreed that a tap at every street corner was a pressing requirement. It took the panchayat two months to arrive at a consensus and communicate its decision to me.

We started planning the project in earnest. I asked the young engineers at ITC who were relatively free to design a water distribution system to provide a tap on each street. It would be serviced by a sump and an overhead tank. Since the company was drawing water for its paper mill, I said about 100 cubic meters of that water could be filtered and supplied to the sump to be constructed inside the village. The total estimated cost of the project was Rs 12 lakh in 1992.

But before beginning the work I wanted to know how much of the funding would come from the panchayat. I was told it had no money to spare. But I insisted that it must pay something failing which I would have to pull out of the project. After much resistance the panchayat finally said it could raise Rs 5 lakh.

I then took the panchayat members to the taluk board president and pleaded their case. 'These people are suffering for want of drinking water. They are prepared to put in Rs 5 lakh. How much can you give?' The president looked at me and wondered if I was a person from the local area. I said that I was from Mysore. He then wondered, 'If you are not from here why are getting into this 'usabari' (concern about a local issue)? You are only supposed to run that factory.'

I told him that I had no choice but to get involved since people were demanding water from ITC. 'As you know, the people run that factory and they need water. That is why I am here.' He thought for a moment and granted us Rs 2 lakh.

I then approached the district collector with a delegation of villagers and the water project proposal. She gave Rs 1 lakh from her emergency fund. We had so far got an assurance for Rs 8 lakh. I sent a detailed project report to my head office seeking a sanction of Rs 4 lakh. It was okayed immediately.

There was happiness all around now that the project was all set to take off. In the days ahead the local community worked day in and day out to construct the sump and the overhead tank. ITC honoured its commitment to draw and filter 100 cubic meters of water and deliver it to the sump. The panchayat executed the project in record time of two months with help from the local community.

The drinking water project earned much goodwill for ITC. Union activity became a lot more subdued at the factory. The company management was seen as being reasonable and well meaning. If anyone made negative remarks about ITC, people would tick them off saying that they should not be complaining when the company was trying so hard to be helpful.

By the time the project was fully operational, Mr J.N. Sapru, chairman ITC, was due for retirement and was visiting Bhadrachalam one last time. When our MD, Mr Chug, told me about the farewell visit I suggested that we get the outgoing chairman to formally inaugurate the water project.

Mr Sapru was excited. 'All my life I wanted to do something for the village, and this is the best thing that can happen,' he said.

The date of the inauguration was fixed, and the preparations were made. But for three days before the event, it started raining cats and dogs in Bhadrachalam. Any arrangements we made in terms of setting up pandals were simply blown away by the stormy weather. The separate arrangements made by the villagers to welcome Mr Sapru were also washed away by the severe and unrelenting downpour.

My MD rang up from Hyderabad and suggested we call off the inauguration. 'Padmanabh, holding a function will not be possible because we hear it will be raining heavily for another three days. We will simply have to cancel it.'

The call had come the previous morning before the scheduled inauguration. I was very disappointed, but I was hoping against hope. 'Sir you give me time till tomorrow morning. You are supposed to start at 10 a.m. Give me till 7 o'clock in the morning. If it is still raining, we will call off the inauguration.' He said he could wait but not beyond the 7 a.m. deadline.

It poured the whole night, and it was still raining when I got up at 3 a.m. with no signs of any let-up. I decided that only divine intervention could help in such circumstances. I took the car and drove to the Lord Rama Temple. At 4 a.m. when the doors opened for the morning puja, I went in. The priests and all those present were surprised to see someone drenched in the rain coming to the temple at that hour.

I prostrated before God and made a fervent plea: 'Many people have worked towards making this function a success. The water project is for the good of the people. Please help us. I can't say anything else, but I need your help.' By the time the morning puja was over it was about 6 a.m. I came out of the temple to be greeted by bright sunshine. The rain had stopped! A miracle had happened. I ran to the nearest phone and called Hyderabad to give the MD the good news.

At Bhadrachalam people became almost delirious because the rain had stopped. Mr Sapru and others came on schedule on three helicopters. People were dancing with joy. The drinking water project was inaugurated by Mrs Sapru. The local merchants' association held a farewell reception for Mr Sapru.

The next morning the visitors left at 10 a.m. Half an hour after their helicopters took off it started raining again. It was as if God had listened to my prayers and put the rain on hold for a day.

Who says miracles don't happen!

Reversing a District Collector's Orders

Being the chief executive of an ITC unit brings with it responsibility and a fair share of problems. One day I got a phone call from the district collector. She said she had received complaints that our factory's pipeline which discharged used water into the Godavari River was leaking heavily at various points and damaging crops in the areas it passed through. She ordered that we take immediate action to stop the leakage in two days and compensate 'farmers' for the crop loss they suffered. If her order was not complied with, she threatened to shut down the factory.

Taken aback by the district collector's instructions, I went to inspect the 5 km pipeline. It was true that there were several leakages, but all the crops had been harvested by the farmers so there was no damage done. I also learnt that the leaks were the handiwork of those who owned land next to the pipeline. Since the discharged water from the paper mill contained fine fibre useful for crops, they were creating openings to access free water containing fibre.

I was further told that the persons complaining to the collector were not farmers but people with vested interests and union leaders who were putting pressure on the ITC management to negotiate for some compensation, including employment for their kith and kin.

I immediately ordered the engineering department to send a crew to seal all leakages within twenty-four hours. I also got 100 security guards from Hyderabad and put them on duty along the pipeline protecting the repaired pipeline in three shifts. I informed the collector of the action taken and sought a meeting with her to respond to the compensation issue.

Two days later the collector rang me up. She was agitated and said, 'Padmanabh, what have you done? There are now many more farmers at my door. They want me to request you not to plug the leaks since it provides essential water for their crops. They have also complained that those who had created a ruckus about the leaks were not farmers, but some local leaders and workers' representatives who wanted to put pressure on the ITC management through me to get some benefits for themselves.'

The collector then asked me to let the leakages be. I insisted that the farmers who had come to get the leakages restored be identified by her office. She could also get their signed appeal for restoration of the water leakage with an undertaking that they would not claim compensation from the company in future.

She promptly ordered her office to do that and sent a copy to me. Following that the special security deployment along the pipeline was withdrawn and sent back to Hyderabad. Soon after the problem had been resolved the collector called me up: 'You are a very intelligent person. You reversed a big problem and sent it back to my doorstep. But I appreciate the swift managerial action you took to protect your company's interest.' I thanked her for her appreciation.

Later, she was the one who released Rs1 lakh for the community drinking water project I piloted.

Finally, Women Power Triumphs

Outside its factory ITC owned a large piece of unused land separated from the campus by the main road leading to Bhadrachalam town. Beyond the company's land were villages. A lone water tap near the main road served the villagers and factory workers living on the other side. The women folk from the villages used to cut across the unused company land to access water from the tap provided by ITC.

But things changed in 1990 when the company decided to construct a building for research into 'Clonal multiplication of

Eucalyptus plants' on the unused land. Prior to the construction of the research centre, ITC began to fence its land which was lying unused.

This led to protests from the villagers and workers' unions since the fencing affected workers who lived beyond the company's unused property. Their principal complaint was that the fencing would deny them the right of way through the unused land to the water tap. This was a privilege they claimed they had enjoyed for decades, and the company was unfair in obstructing their free passage.

The women were the most adamant since the fencing meant they would have to walk a long distance around the fence to collect water every day. A company contractor and the local sarpanch could not convince the people that the land was owned by ITC and therefore it had the right to fence its property. The fencing work had to be halted.

Since there was a deadlock over the issue, as chief executive of the ITC unit, I had to find a solution. Considering that most of the persons to be affected by the fencing were women, I asked the sarpanch to hold my meeting with the agitating women. At the meeting I explained that the company had no obligation to provide water to the villagers, but it had provided a tap near the road as a humanitarian gesture to help the women. If the villagers were adamant, then ITC could discontinue the water supply to the tap, and they would have to fetch water from the Godavari River which was about 5 km away.

I also impressed upon the gathering that no one can force the company to supply water to the villagers. As the women realized the gravity of the situation their attitude changed. They requested me to solve the problem. I suggested that we could lay a pipeline and install a tap near their village so there would be no need to cross the company's land for water. I said the new pipeline would be provided only if the company is allowed to fence its land.

The women felt it was a win-win solution. But instead of one tap, they wanted three to cover the entire village. I agreed to their request. It was only later that I came to know that their plan was to distribute the three taps in such a way that they would be located to serve clusters of houses where members of different castes and religions were living.

As the work of laying the pipeline across the company land began, three unions disowned the agreement with the women's group, claiming that the whole plan was a 'trick played by Padmanabha' and that the water will not be supplied near the residential clusters once the fencing of the company land was completed.

The sarpanch and the contractor met me and suggested that the pipeline work be stopped since the unions had again misled the women's group. I told them to complete the work of installing three taps as agreed, with proper platforms and drainage arrangements.

Once the pipeline work was completed, we allowed the water supply through all the three taps for ten days. Then I stopped the water supply. The women's group approached me and wanted to know why the supply was discontinued. I told them as agreed we had provided water taps near their houses on the understanding that the company's land would be fenced, and construction of the research centre would start. Since the three unions were adamant in stopping the fencing, the women could continue to take water from the lone tap near the road.

The women stood up together and unanimously said, 'Sir you start fencing your land, let us see who can stop it.' When we resumed the fencing work, the workers belonging to the unions came with sticks and stones to disrupt the work only to be confronted by the village women. The men, they said, would have to get water for the family if it had to be fetched from the lone tap near the road.

The workers dispersed after that, and the three new taps started supplying water to the villagers. The company's land was secured with the fencing. Women power, I understood, had triumphed.

Saved From a Naxal Attack by Lord Rama's Grace

The Naxalite movement was very active in Bhadrachalam in the 1980s and 1990s. Several encounters between police and insurgents made news with heavy causalities reported on both sides. As head of ITC's Paper Board Unit, the district police had provided me with security cover. Though we tried to put up a brave front, there was always a nagging fear in the back of our minds that we could be targeted.

I used to regularly receive threatening letters signed 'Annalu' or elder brother, which, incidentally, was how Naxal leaders identified themselves. But many of these notes signed `Annalu' were declared as fake by the local police.

I once received an inland letter signed 'Annalu' which addressed me respectfully as 'Maharajeshri Padmanabhagariki.' In it was the plea that one of the workers of the company who had been denied his well-deserved promotion be promoted and the injustice corrected. I ignored it. A week later another letter followed addressing me less respectfully as 'Sri Padmanabhagariki' and containing the same plea. I ignored that one too. A week later one more letter came addressing me as plain 'Padmanabha' with the same contents as the earlier letters, but with one addition that if action was not taken things could take a serious turn.

When I did not react to it, a fourth letter came which addressed me crudely as 'Ore (hey) Padmanabha' and threatened action if that letter was ignored too. The police to whom these letters were forwarded asked me to ignore the threat, as they were not written in a language typical of a Naxalite communication.

However, a few days later when I was preparing for bed after attending a cultural programme with my wife Uma, son Anand and our friend Chengappa's son Girish, I got a call on the intercom. It was from Srinivas the son of our production manager, Satyanarayana, whose house was adjacent to ours.

I was advised in a hush-hush voice not to come out of the house and to switch off all our lights. Srinivas whispered that their house was surrounded by gun wielding Naxalites. They were asking his father to come out to talk to them and had assured him that no harm would come to him or his family. Satyanarayana was communicating with them from a first-floor window and was trying to persuade them to come to the office next day for a meeting. However, the Naxals were insisting that he meet them just then.

On being apprised of the situation, I called up the junior security officer on duty at the factory gate and asked him to alert the police. But I asked him specifically not to venture on his own to the residential area. But he obviously felt he should investigate and drove in his jeep to where we lived. The five Naxals mistook the vehicle to be a police patrol and jumped over the compound wall and disappeared into the night.

Meanwhile, I called up the SP and DSP of the area informing them about the incident. Both came with adequate police force by midnight, and we met and discussed the incident. They interrogated a few persons and pieced together the sequence of events.

It turned out that four armed men and a woman dressed in khaki had surreptitiously entered the area where the five houses of top ITC executives were located. When the colony maintenance worker came to open the water valves for the five houses, the woman among the five, caught the worker, covered his mouth so that he could not scream for help, and asked him to identify the general manager's house, and the worker had by mistake pointed to Satyanarayana's residence.

This was a miraculous mistake because I could not have conversed or negotiated with the gun-toting group in Telugu as fluently as Satyanarayana did. Anyway, fortunately for us, the gang left before the police came.

Next day the police surrounded the houses around the periphery of the compound wall and interrogated people seeking information about the Naxalites. Following the incident, the inner periphery of the compound wall was further fortified with heavy barbed wire to prevent unauthorized entry of people.

I still sincerely believe that it was Lord Srirama's grace that saved the five families from disastrous consequences. It was, however, unfortunate that the incident led to the police resorting to third degree interrogation of several innocent people living near the periphery of the compound wall.

Father's Good Deed Pays Off 38 Years Later

Engrossed with work at ITC, I was guilty of having relegated personal matters to the back burner. One such issue related to a plot of land I was allotted in 1984 by the Karnataka Housing Board (KHB) in Yelahanka New Town, Bangalore.

Having taken possession of the plot I had not submitted the mandatory plan for construction to the KHB for five years. Suddenly, in 1989, I was served an ultimatum that if I did not submit my house plan and begin construction within one month, my allotment would stand cancelled, and the site would be re-allotted to other deserving applicants. Disturbed by the ultimatum, I rushed to Bangalore from Bhadrachalam having taken just one day's emergency leave.

As soon as the KHB office opened at 10 a.m., I went to meet the secretary in his office. The officer had not come in yet but his personal assistant, Ms Ramamani, a kind and helpful lady asked me the reason why I wanted to see her boss. When I explained with anguish my need to seek more time to construct the house since I was posted in Bhadrachalam, she offered me a chair to sit and asked me to calm down.

She said I need not be so disturbed by the notice I had received but suggested the action I needed to take to prevent any re-allotment of the plot. She advised me to immediately submit a plan for the construction of the house and seek its approval which would give me breathing time of four to six months. Meanwhile, I could begin the construction and seek time for completing the work.

But where was I to get a plan ready at such short notice? When I told Ms Ramamani that I can't stay back in Bangalore to get a proper plan ready and submit it since I had to catch a flight to Hyderabad that night, she smiled and calmed me down again.

She rang up Mr Khan, head of KHB's building plan department, and requested him to arrange a building plan 'suitable for a KHB 50 X 90 site in Yelahanka New Town' She added that the plan should be ready for submission by 3 p.m, the same day.

Mr Khan asked for details of my allotted site and said that he would get the plan ready. Ms Ramamani then gave me a form to be filled up and submitted along with the building plan. When I told her that the plan Mr Khan would prepare may not suit our requirements and that I need to discuss the plan with my wife, she smiled and told me that I could always submit a request to revise the plan citing various reasons. That would give me time to plan my house according to my requirements.

Feeling relieved, I thanked Ms Ramamani and left the KHB office to return by 3 p.m. When I got back, I was directed to meet

Mr Khan, I went up to his office on the second floor and introduced myself. Mr Khan was an elderly gentleman who asked me to be seated and asked me my qualifications and where I worked.

Then he asked me my father's name. When I said it was A.N. Anantharamiah, he turned emotional and asked, 'You mean the previous deputy commissioner of Chikmagalur?' When I confirmed that was him, he rose from his chair, came around and lovingly held me by the shoulder and said, 'What a pleasure you have given me?'

He then asked me about father. When I told him he was no more he was visibly moved. Mr Khan then explained what made him so emotional and narrated an incident that changed his life. In 1952 he was a diploma holder from a poor family in Chikmagalur and had applied for a draftsman's job in the district office. He had appeared for the written exam and the job interview.

While results were awaited, he got inside information that though he had topped the selection list, someone was manipulating the result and that he may not be selected. Distraught by the news, the young Mr Khan sought advice from an elderly friend of the family, who advised him to meet the deputy commissioner in his house when he met members of the public between 9 and 10 am.

The very next morning Mr Khan joined the queue of people wanting to meet the DC. When his turn came, he explained his family background, his academic achievements, and his anguish at being denied a fair employment opportunity. My father apparently calmed him down and said, 'Go to the district office and meet superintendent Murthy this afternoon and tell him that I have sent you. If, as you say, you have topped the list no one can deny you that opportunity. But if you have not, I will not be able to help you because it will then hurt someone more deserving.'

Mr Khan said he met Mr Murthy that afternoon and was excited to receive his appointment letter. Meanwhile what had transpired earlier was that my father called for the file on selection of draughtsmen and found some manipulation had been done to deny Mr Khan his selection. On noticing the mischief being played, my father had suspended two assistants and ordered Murthy to issue the appointment letter the same day.

Narrating how he and his family had benefitted by his crucial meeting with my father, an emotional Mr Khan said, 'Today I am extremely happy to have been given the opportunity to return a small portion of the debt of gratitude I owe him.'

Mr Khan's story reminded me of what I owe to my parents for the values they practiced and the goodwill they bequeathed to their children. Incidentally, Mr Khan and Ms Ramamani took personal interest to protect my interests and helped with my house plans and approvals.

Resigning on Principle and Losing Retirement Benefits

My career graph at ITC Bhadrachalam Paper Boards Ltd was impressive. I joined in October 1987 as general manager (personnel and administration) and was promoted as vice president (operations) within five months in March 1988. My professional journey then on for the next five years at Bhadrachalam was one that was punctuated by several challenges and conflicts which I successfully negotiated and resolved.

By 1992, the industrial conflicts as well as differences with the local community had been sorted out to a great degree and this reflected in improved productivity at the plant. Under my watch the ITC unit at Bhadrachalam also earned considerable goodwill from the people through some of its initiatives and was seen as a company that 'cares' for the people.

However, professional success comes at a price. During the five years I was constrained to live alone at Bhadrachalam, while Uma and the children were roughing it out in Bangalore. The family reunited only during school vacations or when Uma could find time to visit Bhadrachalam.

But as the situation normalised at the ITC plant, I spoke to Mr Kutty, the MD about the problems faced by my family in Bangalore. I made it known to him that I was seeking a transfer to a better location. It so happened that at that juncture the company's expansion plans needed implementation and so I was transferred to Hyderabad as senior vice president (HR) while Malliwal, senior VP (technical) took over the Bhadrachalam operations from me. The transfer enabled my family to shift to Hyderabad.

During the first six months of my moving into my new posting I noticed that both Malliwal and another senor colleague Agarwal were not happy with my success. I also noticed their tendency to encourage subservience among the middle rung and junior managers. Further, I had seen the two charge some of their personal expenses to the company. In fact, once when my approval was sought for endorsing their personal expense as company expense, I had refused to oblige.

In 1993, from the organizational changes taking place, I sensed that there was a move to designate Agarwal as chairman and Malliwal as MD of ITC Bhadrachalam, while Mr Kutty would be moved to Calcutta as director ITC, consequent to Mr Chugh becoming the chairman of the group

Expecting these moves, I met Mr Kutty and offered to resign from the company and relocate to Bangalore, since I did not wish to work under Agarwal and Malliwal. Mr Kutty seemed sympathetic and said that he would discuss the matter with Mr Chugh before responding to my offer to resign. A few weeks later Mr Kutty got back to me. He said he had a discussion with Mr Chugh about my apprehensions and he was told that in the event of the two persons occupying the top positions,

I would be transferred to some other unit of ITC to avoid any embarrassment.

Mr Kutty also asked me to avail of the pre-retirement perquisite of a world tour for me and Uma. Taking his advice my wife and I proceeded on our world tour in late October 1994. After visiting various places across the world, we reached Tokyo by late November. While we were in the Japanese capital, I got a call from Mr Kutty that my prediction had come true and that Malliwal would take charge as MD and Agarwal as chairman in March 1995.

I told him that I could fax my resignation right away. But he dissuaded me from taking such a hasty step and said that we could discuss the matter when I got back to Hyderabad. On my return, Mr Kutty held me back from quitting since he said he had spoken to Mr Chugh and that something would be worked out by February end.

It was around that time that my friend Dr G.K. Jayaram arranged admission for my son Prasanna to a professional course in the US and the visa processing was underway as he was to join college in mid-March. I soon became busy making the financial arrangements for my son's study abroad and my friends Chengappa and Jairaj were of great help.

Meanwhile, the days passed by and there was no indication of my relocation within the ITC group. So, I decided to quit on April 1 and served my one month notice from March 1. Around the third week of March, after both Malliwal and Agarwal had taken charge, a review meeting of all departments was arranged at Bhadrachalam where I had to report on the performance of the HR department.

On the day of the meeting at Bhadrachalam, Prasanna called me from Madras announcing that he had got his US visa. The same morning, Agarwal announced my resignation to a select group of senior managers and recalled my contribution to the company during my tenure. However, later at a meeting of all executives Agarwal vented his resentment towards me, but I did not react.

Meanwhile, Mr Kutty failed to relocate me within the ITC group and Malliwal accepted my resignation. Consequently, I lost all my retirement benefits. Neither Mr Kutty or Mr Chugh kept their promise to relocate me, nor did they show any latitude to review my loss of benefits.

At this juncture Prasanna wanted to cancel his plan to go to the US. I persuaded him to go ahead and assured him that I could take care of the situation at my end despite quitting my job. He was worried because I was indeed in a vulnerable situation but as always there was an unseen divine hand that helped me tide over the difficult phase before and after my relocation to Bangalore.

When I look back, fulfilling the US visa requirements for my son was difficult during my last month in ITC. I had to show a bank balance of at least Rs 10 lakh when I hardly had a few thousand rupees. But our friends Jairaj and Changappa readily agreed to help. The latter broke his fixed deposits and transferred about Rs 4 lakh to my account. And Jairaj entered into a sale agreement with me to buy my house in Bangalore and gave Rs 7 lakh as advance. The funds were given on the understanding that the monies would be refunded as soon as soon as the US visa was okayed.

During my last month in ITC, I was riddled with problems on the family front. Prasanna's US visa had initially created problems with his request being rejected. He phoned me from Madras totally dejected. Suddenly I remembered that Lalitha Nataraj, wife of my friend Prof. Nataraj, worked at the US Consulate in Madras. I succeeded in getting through to her on the phone. After introducing myself, I sought her help to counsel Prasanna who was still in the consulate premises. She was more than happy to help. Prasanna met her and she calmed him down and asked him to try again. She told him one rejection was not the end of the world.

I asked my son to apply again for a visa appointment the following week. US visa rules had it that if an applicant's request were to be rejected twice, he or she had to wait for two years for his next request to be considered. So, it was sensible to make the second attempt as quickly as possible. By the grace of God Prasanna got his US visa the following week on his second attempt.

Earlier my son had also applied for an education loan from Canara Bank in Hyderabad. It was processed and the manager assured us that all requirements for the loan were met and that the loan would be released once the visa was cleared.

Prasanna's ticket to the US from Bombay was booked for a Friday. It was a Tuesday when we met the Canara Bank manager for the release of the loan. He suggested that we take the loan on a Wednesday as Tuesday was inauspicious. But when we met him the following day, we were shocked to hear that the loan application was rejected by the bank's head office since the marks my son had obtained for his second language in his degree examination was below 50 per cent.

Any amount of pleading with the bank's headquarters made no difference. I was left with no option but to pray. Suddenly I remembered Andhra Bank where our company had its account. I had earlier not applied for a loan through this bank to avoid any personal obligation to the company's banker. But now that I was desperate, I called up Andhra Bank's senior manager, Mr Joseph. I told him my problem. He responded positively 'Sir when we are here why are you approaching others. We can process your son's loan application by this evening and release the loan tomorrow.'

To ensure his departure on Friday my son and I rushed with his papers and met Mr Joseph. He received us very cordially, scrutinized the documents, took my son and my signatures, and opened Prasanna's Andhra Bank account. He asked us to come and collect the loan sanction order the next morning and draw the necessary money in foreign currency.

Greatly relieved we went home. But our struggle was still not over. The next morning when I kept ringing up Mr Joseph at his residence there was no response. When I called him up at the bank a greater shock awaited us. I was told that Mr Joseph's daughter had committed suicide early that morning. I thought it was end of the road for us.

I once again prayed to God. Suddenly I felt compelled to call on Mr Joseph to console him. Finding the address, I reached his residence where everyone was in in a state of utter shock. I hugged Mr Joseph and uttered a few words of consolation. I took leave of him without uttering a word about Prasanna's loan. As I reached my car, Mr Joseph put his arms around my shoulders and said, 'Sir, I have asked our branch manager to ensure completion of formalities and to release foreign exchange to Prasanna by noon today. Don't worry sir.'

I could not believe that a person in such personal distress could still be conscious of his responsibility to fulfil his promise. I cannot but believe that there was an unseen divine hand at work.

Prasanna's study in the US was secured, But Uma and I faced an uncertain future. We returned to Bangalore and looked for a house to rent since our home was under lease to Nagarjuna Constructions whose manager was staying there. When I contacted him, he was magnanimous enough to immediately vacate the house for us. 'Sir, why do you have to rent a house when you have your own house here,' he said.

Fortunately, our other son, Anand, was employed in Bangalore. Yet I was staring at bleak future from the financial point of view. I thought perhaps God was testing if my faith would hold steadfast even when the future looked dismal. Fortunately, I did not slip into despondency or suffer from any guilt that I might have made a grave mistake by quitting my job. In fact, I was convinced that my resigning from ITC was the right decision since continuing for another six months in the company would have scarred my personality till the end of my life.

Meanwhile, I let people know that I was available as a HR and management consultant. While I kept praying for God's help, I was not able to foresee when and from where that help would come my way. Fortunately, I did not have to wait for too long. Six months after I quit, a professor from TISS Bombay, who I had immense respect for, called me with the request that I direct the comprehensive evaluation of the management of the Christian Medical Association of India. It was a two-year project for which I was paid a consultancy fee. Money started flowing in.

A few months later, ITC sent me an SOS to help it resolve a violent HR conflict at its unit in Mantralayam, Andhra Pradesh. Soon there were several other management consultancy assignments that kept me busy.

By the time I hung up my gloves as a management consultant in 2010, my total earnings far exceeded the salary I earned during my working life. My assignments more than compensated the retirement benefits I lost from ITC.

There surely was a divine hand that guided me and an omnipresent force that protected me during those turbulent and uncertain times.

X
Life After ITC

An Innovative Swachch Bharat Solution

As I mentioned earlier, after saying goodbye to ITC, I based myself in Bangalore as a management consultant and managed a steady flow of assignments. In 1998 a very old friend of mine, with whom I had lost contact, got in touch. He had learnt I was a management and HR consultant and wanted me to help his son who had set up an industrial unit making electrical components.

The unit was based in a locality which had a predominantly Christian and Muslim population. I visited the factory once to assess the perceived problems faced by the management and agreed to meet again a week later with my suggestions.

The company's MD phoned me to fix the time for my next visit. Even as he was speaking to me, he raised his voice at someone. 'Don't you have any sense of shame, can't you see God's images in front of you, I will hand you over to police.' I was stunned and taken aback at this sudden burst of anger. A few seconds later, realizing that he was still on the line with me, he profusely apologized saying that his anger was directed at someone urinating against his compound wall.

He was quickly back to his polite self, and we fixed the time for our meeting later in the day. I went to the factory and after concluding our discussions on the agenda for the day, I asked the MD the reason for his outburst in the morning.

The problem, he explained, was that since his house was on the side of the road, men found it convenient to urinate against his compound wall. They soon turned his wall into a public urinal and the stench that emanated from outside was unbearable. So, he had to routinely shout at the people stopping by to ease themselves.

He then thought he could solve the problem by getting his wall painted with images of various Gods. He felt that this would dissuade people from misusing his wall out of reverence and fear. So, he had his entire wall facing the street, painted with images of Ganesh, Lakshmi, Shiva etc. However, he was frustrated to find that despite that the nuisance continued. After narrating his problem, he wondered if I could suggest a solution.

Having noted that majority of the population in the area were non-Hindus, I realised that the pictures of Hindu Gods would not act as a deterrent. And then I wondered why use images of any God of any religion to serve such a petty purpose.

Therefore, I suggested that he erase the images and paint the entire wall with a grey tint and fix reflecting glass sheets in place of the gods. The MD was sceptical about my idea, but since it was not a very expensive, he implemented it.

Soon after completing the exercise, he called me up to thank me profusely. He said the nuisance had stopped. My simple solution had succeeded as a deterrent because the glass fixed on the wall had transformed it into a large mirror of sorts. And no one wanted to be seen by passers-by while they relieved themselves!

A `Surgical' Dilemma

Travelling frequently between Bangalore, Hyderabad, Delhi, Calcutta and Trivandrum as a management consultant started taking its toll. I started developing neck pain which would become severe at times.

I had first ignored it but in 1999 I finally decided to put my neck in the hands of a renowned surgeon known to the family. After conducting several medical tests and procedures, I was advised that an operation was unavoidable.

The surgeon explained that due to ageing and the strain of frequent travel, the nerves in the neck and bones had become weak, Hence, a surgery at the back of the neck to strengthen the bones and nerves would be an appropriate solution. Since the matter involved the neck, I decided to take a second opinion to help me decide whether I should opt for surgery or not.

Therefore, I sent my tests results to a neurosurgeon in the family for his advice. After examining my papers—medical tests, x-rays, MRI scan etc.— the family surgeon concurred with the earlier advice given to me. But he recommended that the operation be done from the front of the neck instead of the back as recommended by the first surgeon.

Confronted by the two conflicting approaches, I referred the issue to my brother Dr Sampath Kumar, a heart specialist at AIIMS, New Delhi. His immediate response was not to do anything till he got back to me.

He referred the problem to his close friend, a neurologist. After a thorough examination of all the test reports, the neurologist in Delhi and my brother concluded that no surgery was needed. Instead, they recommended that I sleep without a pillow under my neck or use a very thin pillow to support my head. I followed their advice, and the neck pain disappeared in about three weeks. Even today I sleep on a very soft and thin pillow and my neck is pain free

Often simple answers work better than complex solutions.

Tale of Two 'Khatas'

In 2010, my son Anand bought a property outside Bangalore, which came under the jurisdiction of the revenue office in Singanayakanahalli village. To ensure the title of the property was on his name a *khata*—a government document that recognizes the ownership of property or land—had to be obtained. After several visits to the panchayat office, I was unable to contact the 'village accountant.'

So, I went from my residence in Yelahanka early one morning and waited along with others for the accountant. When the gentleman arrived, everyone rushed to meet him. I waited my turn patiently. When I finally caught his attention, he asked me what I wanted. I told him that I needed a khata and gave him the documents. He said, 'You have to pay the backlog of land taxes and it will cost you Rs10,000.'

I showed him all the tax receipts. He looked at them and pronounced 'You will then have to pay Rs 5,000.' I asked him whatever for since the taxes due to the village were already paid. He turned to me and smiled. I got his message. So, I asked him in a loud voice for everyone to hear, 'Lunchana (bribe), that's what you want?' All those present were astonished at my audacity.

The man smiled but was red faced. Then I said it loud and clear, 'Look I won't pay any bribe to anyone. If you hold back my khata and call me here a hundred times I will come, but you will get no bribe. Give me an acknowledgement for the application I have submitted.' He sheepishly gave me the acknowledgement.

Those assembled at the panchayat office reverently made way for my exit from the office. As I reached my car, I saw the accountant come running to me. He pleaded: 'Sir, please give me your address and phone number. Please don't take the trouble to come to this office, I will deliver the khata to you by this evening or tomorrow morning.' He came to my house the same evening and delivered the document.

But my headache was far from over. Since the property also fell under the jurisdiction of the Bruhat Bengaluru Mahanagara Palike (BBMP)—the administrative body responsible for providing civic amenities in the Greater Bangalore metropolitan area—another khata was needed to pay taxes to the BBMP. That proved to be an uphill task with red tape and official apathy to be negotiated.

My struggle to get the papers processed at the BBMP was such that it even attracted media attention. Reproduced here is the text of a story which appeared in the *New Indian Express* on September 19, 2017:

'81-yr-old gets Khata after 85 days

His efforts began during end of June, and he finally got the khata on Sept 16

By Tushar Kaushik

Express News Service

BENGALURU: An 81-year-old citizen was made to run around for almost three months to get a khata for his son's property, laying bare the BBMP's inefficiency and apathy. The citizen made 25 visits to four BBMP offices, made 81 calls and sent 22 emails to officials concerned over a staggering 85 days. He even tried to contact Chief Minister Siddaramaiah in between but could not meet him.

Padmanabha Arkalgud wanted to obtain a khata (a revenue document containing a property's details needed to pay property tax) for his son's property at Nagarjuna Meadows 2, Doddaballapur Road, Yelahanka. He began his efforts during the end of June, and finally got the khata on September 16. The initial delay was caused by a rule by which all khatas for any apartment or gated community is to be issued at once. In this case, the builder had only applied for khatas for 200 out of 450 flats about four years ago.

Referring to this rule as 'unreasonable', Arkalgud said, "On explaining that this order causes unfair problems to tax-paying owners who are made to wait for no fault of theirs, the Joint Commissioner advised me to send an email representation and said he would resolve the problem." Arkalgud sent the email on July 17.

What followed was a nightmare for the 81-year-old as he was made to wait without any response for several days at a stretch. During this time, he met BBMP Joint Commissioner M Venkatachalapathy, and sent emails to BBMP Commissioner N Manjunath Prasad and Mayor Padmavathi G. He even contacted the Chief Minister's office and tried to meet him but could not do so. When he once called revenue inspector Babu to enquire, the latter replied, "Yours is not the only work we do here. I have to finish 250 documents. You must understand. We will tell you when it is done."

There were some good officers too, like ARO Lokmata, who tried her best to accelerate the process. However, she had to take medical leave in between, which slowed down the process. The final push was also given by her, after which Arkalgud finally got the khata on September 16.

Thanks to Arkalgud's unrelenting pursuit, most of the remaining 250 applications of the apartment were processed to be released. Arkalgud consciously did not attempt to bribe anyone and had himself organised khata melas at Yelahanka New Town. He said, "The series of incidents clearly highlights the passive nature of the officials who routinely pass the buck, with no fear of being held accountable or even questioned."

A senior revenue official said the rule of issuing khatas collectively had largely delayed the process. However, even after its resolution, Arkalgud had to wait for one-and-a-half months. The official added that the revenue officials had lot of other work too, including collection of property tax, removal of illegal hoardings and work for the upcoming state elections. BBMP Commissioner Manjunath Prasad acknowledged that he was aware of Arkalgud's plight.

Toilet Gotra

In May 2019, S.V.S. Rao, the retired general manager of RBI Bangalore, and a friend for over 60 years, noticed the pathetic plight of toilets at the Government Primary School in Byrasandra in Jatanagar, Bangalore. He could not bear the unkempt sight of the toilets and the stench that emanated from them. Rao got in touch with me and wanted my help in solving the toilet problem of the school.

He was very right about the pathetic state of the toilets. As many as 160 students (90 girls and 70 boys) were using them. Other than the horrible condition of the toilets, the doors of the stalls were all broken. Indeed, things had come to such a pass that girl students had to stand guard outside the toilet while one of them went inside.

When Rao and I went to have a look, we decided to demolish and create hygienic toilets at the same premises through crowd funding. Getting swiftly into action, we photographed the toilets and sent an appeal for contributions through email and WhatsApp to all our friends and relatives.

We also opened a savings bank account at Andhra Bank in which we were joint account holders. Contributions were to be sent to that account. The money started coming in slowly but surely.

Both Rao and I were keen to perform pooja at the nearby Ganesh Temple before starting the renovation of the toilets. When we went to the temple, the chief *Archak* (priest) asked us our gotra (lineage). I said, 'Toilet Gotra', which he found amusing. Then we explained our project. To our surprise the Archak pointed out that all the priests of the temple were pooling money to help poor children buy books, uniforms and pay their school fees.

He then announced that since our project was to help children, he would like to contribute some money from the temple trust. We were surprised when he donated Rs 31,000. With humility we accepted the money as Lord Ganesha's contribution.

A reporter of the *Deccan Herald* picked up our story in which he highlighted how two octogenarians were determined to provide hygienic toilets to students of a government-run primary school. Once the report was published, the response to our appeal for financial support grew exponentially. Our colleagues from the last 30 years suddenly came on board and contributed. One person from Bombay whom neither of us knew, chipped in with Rs 50,000.

With money in the kitty, we approached construction contractors who quoted about Rs 3 lakh for the project. Our own assessment was that the job could be done within Rs 2 lakh. Therefore, we hired Rao, a labour contractor, and arranged for the materials needed and personally supervised the renovation work,

It was completed in about three weeks at a cost of Rs 1.76 lakh which included fixing steel doors, ceramic toilet fittings, tiles, a storage tank and fresh plumbing work. Since the contributions that came in was over Rs. 3.5 lakhs, we brought some furniture needed by the school with part of the surplus funds. But even after that we still had some money left.

On completion of the Byrasandra Project, the opening ceremony was held in the presence of the local MLA and some donors. One of them, the Inner Wheel of the Rotary Club came forward to take responsibility for regular maintenance of the renovated toilets.

As we were still left with surplus funds, we received requests from two other government primary schools, located at Sarakki and Bandepalya to renovate their toilets, which were over 25 years old. At Bandepalya, a local philanthropist had renovated the boys' toilet, but had left the toilet for girls untouched. So, the school management had asked the girls to use the renovated toilet and the boys were asked to use the surrounding fields. Rao and I visited both the schools and assessed the funds required for renovation and realized that we were short of Rs 63,000.

We sent out another appeal on email and WhatsApp with a detailed status report, mentioning funds received, details of payments made and surplus cash in hand. We noted that to help the two schools required another Rs 63,000. Funds came in but as we started the work, we realised we were still short of Rs 23,000.

In yet another appeal we sent out, it was underlined that the renovation work would be limited by the funds available as on October 3, 2019. A donor from the US immediately transferred Rs 23,000 to our account.

We began work without losing time. Meanwhile, *Deccan Herald* carried yet another report on our efforts in the two schools. It even posted a video story online on how two senior citizens were sweating it out to provide hygienic toilets at two more government schools in Bangalore. The reports further encouraged people to support our cause.

Money is still flowing at the time of writing this. Meanwhile, two more electronic media organisations—one from Bangalore and the other from Delhi—want to cover our effort. Hopefully that will translate into more money for the cause.

One lesson that came through loud and clear was that if there is a sound social cause, people are willing to join hands and contribute. But those initiating any crowd funding drive for a just cause must live up to the trust reposed in them and must be transparent in their dealings and completely dedicated to the cause they espouse.

Launching the Yelahanka New Town Citizens' Forum

When we moved into Yelahanka on the outskirts of Bangalore in the 1990s, one of my initiatives became an important contribution to civic life in that suburb. I felt the need for a citizens' collective to deal with civic problems, cleanliness and law and order and began mobilising residents in this regard. I visited over 1000 homes to secure participation of all residents, most of whom responded enthusiastically. Thereafter, I called a meeting in the local park and invited policemen for an interaction with residents. The meeting led to a significant decision in regard to citizen participation in night patrols undertaken by the police. It was resolved that every male resident would join the night patrol once a month. I sat with fellow residents and drew up a monthly night patrol chart, which most residents adhered to. The enthusiasm of the residents to secure their neighbourhood inspired the local police as well and the work of the joint vigilance squads resulted in a drastic drop in the crime rate in Yelahanka New Town.

I later moved out of that neighbourhood, but the citizens forum continues to flourish ensuring better living conditions for the residents and improved civic amenities.

XI
Around the World

From Guntur and Beyond

It was while I was based in Guntur and just before I ended my stint with the National Tobacco Company in 1981 that I went on my first trip abroad. As commercial manager I was deputed to be present in Tokyo for the final inspection of the tobacco exported by us.

Since we knew the date of the inspection two months in advance, I had to apply for my passport. I asked my wife Uma to also get her travel documents ready so that if it was possible, she could accompany me. She refused to apply for her passport saying that unless her trip was cleared by the company she did not wish to go through the entire rigmarole. 'What will people think if I get the passport made and I don't go, it will be so funny,' she said, and I had no counter to that.

The company released Rs.15,000 for my ticket and expenses for the five-day trip. I had to go to Madras to get the Japanese visa. While in the city I saw a travel agency promoting an 'around the world in 90 days trip' for Rs 9000. That aroused my curiosity. So, I made enquiries and found out that Pan Am was offering tickets for the trip for just Rs 9000.

As per the scheme, the airline would issue 16 travel coupons for Rs 9,000. The first coupon would be marked 'exit Bombay' and the sixteenth coupon marked 'return Bombay.' You could travel in one direction till the last return coupon. The rest of the coupons were all blank. So, you go to Bombay and book your seat on any Pan Am flight to any destination. If a seat was available, you were put on the flight and off you go!

Impressed by the scheme I brought the coupons out of the Rs15000 the company had advanced. Then I went to the American consulate seeking a US visa for which I was asked to register and come back the following day. It was promptly issued

I returned to Guntur and sought one month's leave before the inspection in Tokyo. That done I planned my world tour with a return via the UK. Pan Am's 16 coupons, I thought, were most convenient and flexible to travel freely across the world.

Before embarking on my trip, I told the travel agent to somehow arrange a passport for Uma quickly and keep a tab on places where I would be. The agent could simply call up the telephone numbers I had given to inform me if my wife's passport was ready.

With all the travel documents ready I found myself at Bombay airport. I went to the Pan Am desk to check in for the flight leaving for Bangkok, my first stop on the trip. The person at the desk directed me to proceed for immigration clearance. The man at the counter saw my documents and declared that I could not travel because my passport didn't have the 'immigration clearance not required' stamp. It was a rule introduced just about a month earlier by the government which neither I nor the travel agent was aware of.

Though I pleaded fervently I was not given immigration clearance. I showed the officer the letter from Japan, I told him that my ticket would become useless if I did not start my trip but to no avail. 'No, we can't allow you to travel. That is the rule,' I was told.

This meant my whole trip was gone. The coupons I bought for Rs. 9000 would get cancelled as there was no refund on such promotional schemes. More importantly the tobacco inspection in Tokyo and the export contract could go for a toss without the presence of the supplier's representative. I felt horrible and approached other officers in immigration but each one of them said they could not help.

In desperation I asked them to give me the telephone number of their chief. At midnight I rang him up and explained my problem. He said, 'Look, I don't know who you are, and I don't quite understand your problem. In any case I can't tell the officers at the airport over the telephone to let you go. It is up to you to convince them. If they are convinced you can go, otherwise you can't.' He put the phone down.

Not knowing what to do, I sat down and stared at the roof in the immigration area feeling lonely, lost, and insecure. Suddenly there was pat on my shoulder and I turned around. It was Mr Kulkarni, the superintendent of immigration. 'Young man, what is bothering you? Why are you staring at the roof? he asked.

I told him that it felt as if the roof was collapsing on me. Then I narrated my problem. He asked me for the letter inviting me for the inspection in Japan and then enquired about my educational qualifications. 'I have passed B.Sc. BL, and I have done my MS from the Tata Institute of Social Sciences, Bombay,' I promptly replied.

'Oh, from the Tata Institute of Social Sciences! That is very impressive,' he said and then added much to my relief that he would let me go. With that he signed my immigration clearance.

I was grateful and overwhelmed. 'Mr. Kulkarni, I am seeing God in you,' I said.

'You don't have to say all that. Go and enjoy yourself. This rule came only very recently so we can exercise discretion in some cases and your credentials are good and hence I am allowing you to go,' he said matter-of-factly.

'Sir, after the trip I will be returning via Bombay. Can I bring you a small souvenir from abroad to express my thanks?' I enquired

His response stunned me. He simply said, 'Yes, I want you to bring me a souvenir. You know what? You come back with a smile, that is the best souvenir you can get me. Bon voyage, all the very best at the inspection in Japan.'

When I look back, I am convinced as I was then, that it was God who appeared before me as Mr Kulkarni!

A 'Purified' Vegetarian Meal in Bangkok

After Mr Kulkarni cleared my immigration obstacle in Bombay, I caught the flight to Bangkok where I was to meet Mr Matsushita, the regional manager of the Japan Tobacco Company, stationed in Thailand.

As I came out of the arrival terminal at Bangkok airport, I saw that Mr Matsushita had personally come to receive me. He dropped me at the hotel where I was booked for my two-day stay and said he would be back to take me out for dinner.

He later returned with one of his colleagues and we drove to a restaurant. While we talked business, Mr Matsushita gave me the menu card seeking my choice of food. What was listed on the menu was so strange to me that I requested my host to choose what he thought would be close to Indian preparations and taste. Mr Matsushita promptly ordered some rice preparations, with salads.

But when the food came, he suddenly realized that I was a vegetarian. So, he turned to the waiter, 'Joe I forgot, my guest is a vegetarian. He can only eat vegetarian food.' Joe said that it was not a problem. He held up the serving dish with the rice preparation and with tongs he removed all the meat pieces. He then declared with a twinkle in his eyes, 'Here is your vegetarian meal.'

Mr Matsushita didn't know what to say. To save my host from embarrassment, I said, 'It's okay. I will take out even the little pieces.' I then ate the 'purified vegetarian' meal. I reckoned I could make this cultural concession and remembered my mother, a strict vegetarian, feeding me chicken soup sans pieces of meat when I was young to save me from a severe medical condition that weakened my bones.

The following day we were to go on a trip during which I got an opportunity to learn an aspect of Japanese culture. Mr Matsushita had sent a car to pick me up and take me to his house from where we were to go to a particular office later. At his house I gave him and his wife some souvenirs from India. We greeted each other with traditional bows as is the Japanese custom. Then Mr Matsushita said we could now leave.

As we walked towards his car his wife followed and Mr Matsushita said he had to drop his wife at the market. I said that was perfectly fine by me and went to sit in the front seat next to the driver. I noticed Mr Matsushita was agitated. He patted me on my shoulder and said, 'No, no you come and sit at the back with me.'

I pointed towards his wife indicating that she should be sitting beside him. He said 'No, no, no, we Japanese don't do that. The guest has to sit with the host. You come and sit next to me.' I felt rather embarrassed seeing Mrs Matsushita sitting in the front seat next to the driver. She got dropped off on the way.

Later when I thought about it, I accepted it as part of Japanese culture where guests get precedence even over ladies. That is their cultural protocol which I had to respect.

In Paris Without a Visa!

Because she was initially reluctant to apply for her passport, my wife Uma got her travel documents ready only when I had almost completed the tour of the US with the UK next on my itinerary. So, she flew from India to England and then headed to Scotland where she stayed with her sister Leela near Edinburgh till I joined her there.

We went around Scotland enjoying the picturesque landscape and landmarks courtesy Leela and her husband Gadadhar. But we were restless and had more places—in fact countries—in mind that we wished to explore. Uma's passport was endorsed with visas for UK, France and Netherlands. I had visas for USA, UK, Germany and Netherlands. We spotted the mismatch and approached the German consulate in Edinburgh, where after lengthy probing by an official on why Uma had not obtained a visa for Germany in India, he cleared her visit to Germany. At that stage, we had no plans to go to Paris, hence I did not seek a French visa in Edinburgh.

After a week, in Scotland we left for London where we ventured out on a day's sightseeing trip of the British capital. While waiting to board the bus for the city tour, I spotted a signboard outside a travel agency announcing a 'To Paris and back in 2 days' offer for 30 pounds per person. On a whim I suggested to Uma, 'Why not we go to Paris?'

'But you don't even have a visa to enter France,' she pointed out. 'It is okay,' I said, 'we will get into the bus and as we reach the French border, we will seek a transit visa, pay the fee, and head to Paris,' I must add that I was rather adventurous on that holiday! Anyway, when we enquired with the travel agent, he said that my idea was indeed workable.

We went on our tour of London and soaked in the sights and sounds of the city. Uma was not comfortable with the non-veg flavours in London restaurants, so she survived on fruit juice, coffee, and biscuits during our city tour.

Returning to the bus terminal, we simply boarded the bus to Paris! It took us to Dover, in south-east England which was also a major port for ferries across the English Channel to Calais in France. At Dover, our bus drove onto the ferry.

Since Uma had not eaten much during the day, I went to the ferry's cafeteria and asked for 'anything vegetarian?' The guy at the counter said he didn't know what I meant by vegetarian, but he could offer me finger chips. I bought a big plate full and when I gave it to Uma, I saw her face light up She was hungry and she wiped the plate clean.

The bus was offloaded after we crossed the Channel and the journey continued. Tired after an exhausting day we dozed off. Next thing we knew we were in Paris, and I had no French visa! I reassured Uma, 'It is okay we will work out something, but first we must find a hotel to stay.' We did locate a small establishment where the friendly fellow at the counter said 'It is now about 9 o'clock. If you check in right away, you will have to pay for today since rents are calculated for twenty-four hours starting at 12 noon. If you just look around the city and come back in about three hours, you can check in for a day and check out tomorrow noon.'

I thanked him for his advice and then wondered if we could freshen up. He said we were most welcome. So, we used the restroom and returned to the reception area. The chap at the counter enquired if we wanted to book a room in advance. I almost agreed but then I suddenly realized that if he looks at my passport and finds that I don't have a French visa he might ring up the police. Hence, I said, 'No, we will just go around a bit and come back at noon'

We left the hotel and went to see a museum or two. We walked lugging our luggage through an unfamiliar city. Every time I saw a policeman, I felt like hiding behind Uma. I didn't know what would be in store for me if a cop asked me for my papers.

Various possibilities loomed in my mind. I could see myself being dragged to the police station. That would leave Uma having to fend for herself in Paris. There was no end to negative scenarios that my mind conjured up that day. Suffice to say that I trudged the streets of Paris fearing imminent arrest.

Finally, I summoned the courage to make the most of it and decided to see the Eiffel Tower and then go back to England. So, we found our way to the Eiffel. We stood before it in awe. I wanted to go up, but Uma said she feared heights. So, I asked her to wait with our luggage and yours truly rode up the elevator to the top of the tower.

For some reason, when I reached the top and the elevator door opened there were 40 to 50 policemen outside. I did not know what happened to me but when I saw them, I quickly turned back to the elevator and went down. Without taking any further risks we decided to head back to London.

We somehow found our way to the bus stand. The same bus was there with the same driver. I bought two tickets and when we started moving, I heaved a sigh of relief.

But our troubles were not over yet. Before we reached the French coast, the bus stopped, and a man came checking passports. He was the French immigration officer. I closed my eyes and prayed to God for help.

He looked at Uma's passport and gave it back to her indicating that it was okay. The he asked for my passport and went through it twice. Very sheepishly and with an innocent expression, I asked him if he was looking for the French visa. When he replied in the affirmative, I said, 'I am sorry. It is not there.'

'What do you mean it is not there?' he asked raising his voice.

I explained in my best innocent and polite voice, 'Look, last night we came by this very bus. At the border I thought I could get a transit visa. But there was nobody there and I went back to sleep. When I opened my eyes, to my shock, I was in Paris. So, we are just returning without seeing anything because I don't have a visa.' He gave me a stern look and with steely eyes he simply said, 'Next time you come, come with a visa' and gave me back my passport.

I thanked God. The Almighty had once again saved me.

I must add that such an adventure is unthinkable in today's world where cross-border visitors are carefully monitored and entering a country without a visa would land you behind bars. But I was lucky that I survived a day in Paris without a visa!

The Air India Baggage Challenge

After we got back to London from Paris, I was to take the flight to Bangalore, via Germany. Then I realized that my ticket was on Pan Am and Uma's was on Air India. So, I went to the Pan Am office and requested the booking executive to do something. 'Look, my wife and I have to travel to Frankfurt and then on to Bombay. We are booked on different airlines. Can you please transfer my ticket to Air India if it is possible?'

He said he could try if Air India agreed. We were once again lucky, and I got a booking on the evening flight to Frankfurt by Air India. But when I studied the ticket, it dawned on me that the checked in baggage permitted on Air India was only 20 kgs and the hand baggage allowed another 5 kgs. On Pan Am right through my travel I had carried two large suitcases. There was also no cap on the weight of the hand baggage allowed except its size.

Since I was flying Air India. I knew its baggage rules would apply, and we would not be allowed beyond the prescribed limit. This posed a serious a problem since I had gone berserk in buying souvenirs, clothes, chocolates, and gifts without a care because of the liberal Pan Am baggage rules. Now the challenge was to think of a way my wife and I could fit in all our luggage in two 20 kg suitcases and two 5 kg bags, which we were allowed as hand baggage.

This literally called for an out of the suitcase solution! This is what we did. I took out four heavy coats and jackets, four trousers, and five shirts and wore one over the other and filled the pockets with small but heavy souvenirs to reduce the total weight in the two suitcases to less than 21 kgs each. Fortunately, there were no body scans and frisking those days.

I also organised a big plastic bag from the hotel and carried it to the airport. Our hand baggage was also overweight, so I asked Uma to sit in one corner and transfer most of the heavy articles from the handbags and put it into the plastic bag and keep it with her.

After our bags went through checks and came back, she filled all the stuff from the plastic bag back into the hand baggage and boarded the flight. Uma also wore several layers of sweaters and carried a few shawls in her hand. As I walked towards the aircraft, I perhaps looked like a zombie, sweating inside my layers of heavy clothing though the temperature outside was minus 7 degrees Celsius. In fact, I must have been a big body with an unmatched starry-eyed face!

On boarding the flight, it was an ordeal fitting into my seat and wearing the seat belt, but I endured the discomfort till we landed in Frankfurt. My friend D. Ramesh received us at the airport and as I wobbled, he exclaimed, 'Paddi how come you have become so bulky since I saw you last!' I asked him to wait till we got to his house. Once there his wife Indu was awe stuck to see me so bloated. I asked them to wait for an explanation for my girth.

After a cup of coffee, I started taking off my outer clothing. The over coats, jackets and the extra shirts came off till I was left with the last layer of clothing. I suddenly shrunk in size. Both Ramesh and Indu could not believe the strategy we had successfully employed to overcome Air India's 'baggage challenge'. We all had a good laugh over that.

We spent two wonderful days with Ramesh and his family in Frankfurt and then began our ordeal of dressing up for the last lap of our journey to India. At Bombay, my brother-in-law Anantharamiah came to receive us. He was astonished to see me. 'Oh, Paddi, what happened? You have put on so much of weight,' he said. I told him to wait and see.

When I reached his home, my sister Lakshmi was also surprised at my girth. Then I repeated my Frankfurt act of peeling off the layers of clothing. Lakshmi laughed her head off till tears came to her eyes. She continued laughing intermittently the whole day while recalling my peculiar ways of meeting challenges.

An Angel in Beijing

In 2017, I was on my way to North Korea via Beijing. On arriving in the Chinese capital, I and other fellow passengers were picked up from the airport by representatives of Koryo Travels which had arranged our trip to North Korea.

We were first taken to the office of the travel agency in Beijing. Those going to North Korea the next day were asked to assemble in a hall. There were nearly 60 of us from all over the world including the US, UK, Australia, Africa, Sweden, and Indonesia. I was the only traveller from India. We were given detailed instructions for our trip to North Korea. These included the following:

*We would have to leave behind everything related to South Korea we may be carrying—literature, propaganda material, photographs, videos and currency.

*A printed slip marked visa to North Korea would be attached to our passports. There would be no stamping of passports.

*Travellers should stick to the group they are designated to throughout the North Korean tour. They must communicate only through the North Korean guides accompanying their group.

*Photography is prohibited except in designated places.

*At the conclusion of the visit any unused North Korean currency must be returned. It cannot be carried back.

We were then told to proceed to our hotels and to assemble the following morning at 7 a.m. at the travel agency office from where we would be taken to the airport to catch our flight to Pyongyang, the North Korean capital.

No taxi driver was willing to drop me to my hotel since it was a very short trip. Finally, a woman rickshaw driver obliged, and I heaved a sigh of relief. The next morning, I left the hotel by taxi having shown the driver the travel agency's address. He dropped me at a particular point and insisted that it was the place mentioned in the address I had shown him.

Before me all I could see was a six-lane highway with a high pedestrian overbridge. There was no Koryo Travels office in sight. To make matters worse my mobile phone was defunct since I did not have a SIM card valid internationally. I felt totally lost and did not know how to contact the travel agency. I requested people passing by to allow me to use their phone. No one seemed to be willing to oblige. I suppose they could not understand what I was saying since I was speaking in English.

It became very frustrating, and my anxiety grew as time ticked by. Under the circumstances I thought the only recourse was to pray to God. And that I did. After a while looking lost and stranded, I noticed a well-dressed lady walking briskly in my direction. I guessed she may be a company executive who possibly spoke English. I gingerly approached her saying 'Excuse me' and was relieved to hear her respond with a 'Yes?'

Suddenly I felt I was in the presence of God. I poured out my plight to her and sought her help. She took the Koryo Travels number from me and spoke to the manager, asking him where I was supposed to report. She told me that I had to use the overbridge and cross the six-lane highway to the other side to reach the group assembled there. Incidentally, the travel agency manager pleaded his inability to spare any staff to help me haul my luggage across the bridge.

Understanding my plight, the lady picked up my big suitcase and went up the steps leading to the overbridge and asked me to follow with my hand baggage. I was humbled by her gesture. As I started walking up, this angel of a lady, went up fast, kept the big suitcase on top of the stairs and walked down halfway and carried my handbag also to the top. She then took my big suitcase across the bridge and came halfway to help me reach the ground-level on the other side. She then pointed to the spot where the Koryo bus was waiting.

I just looked at her awe struck and unable to express my gratitude in words, but my face probably said it all. Looking at my grateful expression, she patted me with a smile and disappeared up the stairs of the overbridge.

Such voluntary and helpful gestures by strangers changes our perception of foreigners about whom we may carry totally unfounded negative thoughts. That angel in Beijing reinforced my belief in humanity and the omnipresence of God.

My North Korean Daughter

After we arrived at Pyongyang airport all tourists to North Korea were ushered into the customs and immigration lounge. Compared to other international airports, the one at Pyongyang was small with very few aircrafts in sight. But the presence of the military was very visible and formidable.

The immigration form to fill was rather lengthy, seeking details of countries we visited earlier, purpose of our visit to North Korea, amount of foreign currency on our person etc. Once we cleared immigration, our passports were retained by the authorities. They would be returned to us at the time of departure.

We then came out of the airport and boarded a designated bus which would take the group I was in, to our hotel. It was around 7 p.m. There was an English-speaking woman guide and four other men in-charge of our group of about 20 tourists. I noticed that our photographs were printed on a sheet of paper and pasted inside the bus. It resembled the KD (known depredator or criminal) list on the notice boards of Indian police stations.

We were informed by the woman guide that all of us in the group would have to travel and stay together during the four-day trip. We would be taken around in the same bus by the same five persons (including the driver) tasked to take care of us through the trip. As we made our way to the hotel, she told us briefly about the places we would be visiting over the next four days and the precautions to be observed. She particularly emphasised that tourists needed to be guided on moving around and when taking photographs.

At the hotel we were given our room keys with the advice that after freshening up we should proceed to the dining hall for dinner. We were further told to be ready by 7 a.m. next morning to begin the day's tour after breakfast. Wanting to be woken up at 5.30 a.m. I went to the reception to ask for a wake-up call. But none of the hotel staff could understand what I was trying to say because they did not speak English. Suddenly, one of the male guides accompanying us made a beeline towards me and asked, 'What is the matter with you?' He meant what is it that I wanted.

I then realized then that our movements were being closely watched and the guides accompanying us had to monitor us closely. When I explained I needed a wake-up call, the guide said, 'The hotel does not have such a service, but I will wake you up.'

Later when I came down for dinner, I met our woman guide and enquired if there was a separate table for vegetarians. She said there was and led me to a table. A few more tourists who were vegans joined me. As dinner was being served, I went to a corner to take my insulin shot.

Suddenly, the woman guide came up to me and asked if I was a diabetic. When I said I was, she told me in a serious tone, 'On this tour you are under my care. Please make sure that you take all your medicines without fail and on time.' On seeing my intrigued expression, she explained, 'My father was also diabetic, and he did not take his medicines regularly. He died prematurely. To me you are like my father, and I want to make sure that you take good care of yourself and take your medicines on time.' She then enquired if I carried sufficient stock of medicines till my return to India. This concern for my wellbeing instantly established a rapport between us.

But her concern did not end there. Every day at breakfast, lunch, tea and dinner she would come to my table to ensure that I had taken my insulin shot and other medicines. Her connect with me was deeper than I had reckoned. On the third day of our tour, I was among those who had opted for a helicopter ride over Pyongyang. We were taken to the airport just before lunch time and divided in two batches of ten each.

Since I was in the second batch, we were to have lunch while the first group went on the ride. So, I headed for the table when my guide, who I thought was like my guardian angel, came up to me and asked, 'Where are your medicines?' I realised that I had left them in the bus, which had gone off to the parking area, a short distance from the airport.

I tried to make light of my forgetfulness and jokingly said, 'Today is Friday, my medicine exemption day at lunch.' But my guide did not take it lightly. Before I could realize what was happening, she dragged me by my arm all the way to the entrance gate. Meanwhile, she contacted the bus driver on the phone to locate where his vehicle was parked. At the door, she said 'You stay inside, outside it is too cold for you.'

She then ran to the bus collected my medicine bag and ensured that I took my insulin shot before having lunch. I was deeply touched by her gesture. It almost felt like she was the daughter I never had.

I suddenly remembered the regret I felt whenever I saw the special bond between a father and daughter in families we knew. At least for those four days in North Korea, I was grateful to God for giving me the joy of a daughter's real loving care. Unfortunately, all I could give her as a parting gift was a carved wooden memento of an Indian elephant. She accepted it with a warm smile and a hug.

On a lighter note, I picked up a few North Korean souvenirs on my trip. Among them, hidden at the bottom of my suitcase, were some prohibited North Korean currency. But the most attractive souvenir I carried back with me was toilet paper with a $ 100 dollar bill and the face of the US President printed on it! In North Korea there was no love lost for America.

Resolving a 'Matrix' Problem

I have already mentioned in passing how my mobile had become non-operational in Beijing and the problems I ran into because of that. Well, the sad truth was that I thought I had made all the arrangements to ensure that I would remain connected throughout my trip, but I was tricked by a Bangalore company which failed to deliver the international SIM cards it promised.

The itinerary drawn up for my trip to North Korea saw me fly to South Korea and then to Beijing from where I was booked on a flight to Pyongyang, the North Korean capital. On my return journey to India, I was to visit Hong Kong and Macau. In preparation for the long tour, I contacted the international SIM card provider, Matrix, in Bangalore to ensure I would remain connected throughout my trip.

When I called, a female executive of Matrix picked up the phone and courteously sought details of my travel plan. She said that she would not only arrange for the two SIM cards required, but also two handsets with the different SIMs placed in them to avoid my having to change SIM cards during my journey. Two days prior to my departure she called me up and asked me to pay Rs 4799, in cash at her office.

When I pleaded my difficulty in reaching her office, she gave me her personal bank details and asked me to transfer the amount online. When I enquired why I should transfer money to her personal account, she said she would draw cash and remit it to the company to ensure speedy delivery of the SIM cards and the handsets. Believing her, I remitted the amount through my bank on the same day.

But even on the afternoon before my departure, neither the SIM cards nor the handsets were delivered. So, I contacted the executive again. She confirmed that the SIM cards and the handsets were on the way and would certainly be delivered by the evening. I kept ringing her up several times after that and she kept assuring me that the delivery would reach me. Later that evening my calls to her were not answered and then she switched off her phone.

I proceeded on my trip with my phone with no international connectivity. My attempt to find a workable SIM card in South Korea was in vain since the cards available there was not compatible with my mobile phone. Consequently, I was plagued with connectivity problems through my entire trip.

On returning to Bangalore, I called up the Matrix executive who told me dismissively that she was on holiday and that I should call her a week later. That, I thought, was the limit. Without further ado I filed a complaint of having been cheated by Matrix at the Yelahanka New Town police station.

The police promptly called up the company and asked Matrix to send a representative to the police station and settle the matter with me. The company's response was that it was a technical fault and not a case of cheating, and that one of its officials would come to the police station and explain.

I visited the police station every day but there was no progress in the case. On the eighth day, the inspector seeing me at the station almost every day enquired about my problem. When he learnt that nothing had moved, he called up Matrix and asked its manager to come to the police station by the evening and meet him to sort out the issue.

Two managers from Matrix turned up and met me in the presence of the inspector. I recounted how I had been cheated by a member of the company's staff. I was then asked how the matter could be settled. I demanded a compensation of Rs 50,000 for the risks I faced and the difficulty I went through while travelling abroad. I said that I do not want the money for myself, but Matrix could donate it to the blind school in Yelahanka.

The inspector was touched by my gesture. He asked the Matrix mangers to negotiate and settle the matter in five days. They promised to get back after discussing the compensation with their head office. The company did not respond and ignored phone calls from the inspector even after a week. This angered him. He felt he was being belittled and his authority questioned by the men from Matrix.

The inspector asked me to come to the station the next morning and said he would detail a policeman and a policewoman to accompany me to the Matrix office. He directed me to identify the two managers whom I met in his presence. They would then be brought to the police station along with the women executive against whom I had also lodged a complaint.

Accordingly, I went to the plush Matrix office in the Shivajinagar Commercial Complex. The police personnel accompanying me conveyed the inspector's order to bring the two managers and the woman executive to the police station.

Anticipating trouble, the managers as well as the woman executive tried their best to evade coming with us. But the policeman with me was firm and did not budge. When I suggested that we serve notice and leave, he said that would give the three the chance to escape from Bangalore. He insisted he was duty bound to escort them to the police station.

Finally, the three agreed to come in their vehicles accompanied by the policeman. I was asked to return home and come to the police station when I was called.

Later that evening, I was summoned to the police station. When I reached there, the inspector was not present. But a sub-inspector, in the presence of the three Matrix staff members, told me that the trio had accepted their mistake. But they wished to negotiate the compensation amount with me. He suggested that we sort out the issue in a separate room before the inspector arrives.

We sat down to sort out the compensation issue even as the woman executive broke down in tears. The three pleaded that the amount be reduced since it was to be borne by them personally and that they were sorry for causing me so much trouble. I was not moved but agreed to reduce the amount to Rs 35,000.

We agreed on that and informed the sub-inspector. It was conveyed to him that the amount would be paid the next day. However, they were directed to draw the money immediately using their ATM cards and pay me. The sub-inspector wanted the issue settled right there and then. So, the three went out and soon returned with the cash.

Meanwhile, the inspector arrived and the two managers as well as woman executive were lined up against the wall while I was asked to be seated. The inspector addressed them in the way criminals are spoken to. He told them that since they refused to listen to his advice and took advantage of the respect shown to them a week earlier, he was left with no choice but to act tough.

He then asked the sub–inspector to put the three in lock up and to produce them in court the following morning. The woman executive burst out in tears and the others looked startled. I realized that if the matter went to court, I would have to pursue the case for a long, long time. Therefore, I privately conveyed to the sub-inspector that since the compensation issue was settled, the case may be closed.

As we came out of the inspector's office, the sub-inspector convinced his senior that the case could be closed. I quickly called the secretary of the school for the blind and asked him to come to the police station with a receipt book. The compensation amount—Rs.35000—was donated in cash and the case closed.

The following day the Matrix manager reached me personally to hand over the Rs 4,500 I had paid to the woman executive through a bank transfer. The case was sorted out in a month's time. Hats off to our police!

XII
In Conclusion

At the age of 86 some would say that I have earned the right to grumble. But I will not claim that privilege since I believe I lived life the way I wanted to and therefore have nothing much to complain about. Of course, there were ups and downs along the way, but life also provided me a fair share of challenges and overcoming them gave me an immense sense of achievement and fulfilment.

Typically, my life was peppered with good times and not so good times—moments of optimism as well as disillusionment. I am glad to report that I took them all in my stride to emerge after each experience as a better and wiser human being. What helped me in this endeavour were the values inculcated in me by my parents. They taught me to act with integrity and not to compromise on my values. Credit must also go in good measure to God for not only answering my prayers but ensuring that I could see and think clearly through every crisis I faced.

I know very few life stories are destined to sparkle with worldly achievements that will be remembered by posterity. But I believe every life lived is a distinctly unique experience. The sum of what you have learnt from your parents, siblings, teachers, friends, colleagues, wife and children, from places you have travelled to and people you have met, from success and failure as well as your communion with God and nature is the wealth of wisdom you have acquired over the years.

This wealth can come from any quarter—from a humble domestic help to an erudite professor. It can come from the actions and reactions of people which served as eye openers. Simply put, you learn from each experience and if you can adopt the good and eliminate the undesired you have reason to be pleased with yourself.

It is these learnings acquired over the years that I have shared in the preceding pages. Rather than stand and preach from a pulpit, I have recounted the stories etched in my memory and let them speak for themselves.

Have I achieved everything I set my sights on? Very few mortals can lay claim to having done that. In any case it is human nature to always look for new challenges. That said, there is no point in whinging about what you don't have. I would rather do something that brings a smile to the people around me.

Many of you may be wondering what I have up my sleeve after Antarctica. Well, I am now planning a trip to the North Pole! However, I am not sure when my plans will materialize because there are currently restrictions on ships sailing to the Arctic region since they have to pass through Russian waters. But nevertheless, I am preparing myself mentally and physically for the journey. Should it happen then I will gladly add a chapter and recount my experience...

About The Author

Arkalgud Padmanabha has led a fulfilling and active life full of varied experiences marked by its share of highs and lows. It was indeed a rollercoaster of a ride that saw him actively involve with theatre, face a Naxal threat, handle sensitive labour issues and manage operations at an industrial unit of ITC, a corporate major. In between all this, he travelled the world and at 74—much after he retired—he even summoned the courage to make a trip to the southern-most tip of the world— Antarctica! In fact, he has set foot on all seven continents of the world. His latest visit was to North Korea in 2017.

Born on September 30,1936 in Bangalore, Padmanabha graduated in science and then secured a degree in law. Subsequently, he completed his post-graduation in social research from the Tata Institute of Social Sciences, Mumbai. He initially joined the Central Institute of Public Cooperation under the Planning Commission. Later he moved to Harvard University's Centre for Population Studies, India Project, as a Behavioural Scientist. He then moved on to the corporate sector.

Padmanabha quit formal corporate life in 1993 as Senior Vice President ITC Bhadrachalam Ltd. He subsequently served as a consultant to the Christian Medical Association of India, ITC Ltd, Axiom (USA) and VST Industries Ltd.

Today, at 86, he continues to lead an active life. As a trustee of the Lake Puttenahalli Rejuvenation and Bird Protection Trust, Yelahanka, Bangalore, he was among those instrumental in getting the lake declared as the only bird sanctuary in Bangalore. He has also helped construct toilets in government schools through crowd funding. M.S. University, Baroda, bestowed him the 'National Yougantar Unsung Hero Award' in 2020 for his community service. His mantra is: "One may retire from employment, but one shouldn't retire from Life."

As Luck Would Have It is his first book other than professional publications.

www.ingramcontent.com/pod-product-compliance
Lightning Source LLC
LaVergne TN
LVHW041209150826
845673LV00001B/340

* 9 7 9 8 8 9 2 7 7 2 8 0 8 *